"*The One and Only You!* elegantly normalizes the fears and big emotions** carried by all our tweens! Sievers leans on compassion and clinician expertise as she explains the emotions that can contribute to, or erode, our individual and collective wellness. Teachers, counselors, and parents alike will benefit from the plethora of tools provided in the text. Our young adolescents will benefit from the explicit teaching and loving kindness infused throughout." — **JESSICA SWAIN-BRADWAY, PhD,** Executive Director, Northwest PBIS Network, and author of *Integrating and Enhancing Social and Behavioral Learning Using a Multi-Tiered System of Supports*

"**This is an important book for children, and parents of children.** Sievers continues to display her unique skill of approaching kids on their level and explaining life to them in their language. The pages here dealing with anger alone should be required reading for any child in early adolescence." — **CHARLES R. CROSS,** music journalist and author of nine books including *New York Times* bestsellers such as *Heavier Than Heaven*

"*The One and Only You!* is the road map every kid needs. Rendered with** clarity, funk, wisdom, tenderness, and joy, this book is a celebration of individuality and creativity. . . . It's a user-friendly tool kit of self-reflection and personal empowerment all wrapped up in unconditional love." — **DONNA GAINES, PhD,** sociologist, social worker, and author of *Teenage Wasteland: A Misfit's Manifesto* and *Why The Ramones Matter*

"**As a successful professional actor and creative person, the two sure** things I needed growing up were a healthy self-esteem and the can-do attitude for forging my own successful creative path in life. This book helps connect the dots through excellent real-world examples and engaging workbook moments to help record thoughts and move through emotions carefully, which helps unpack and navigate the sudden flooding of emotions and thoughts that happen while growing up. It's a private guidebook to becoming your true self. Where was *The One and Only You!* when I was growing up? What a much-needed book!" — **LEONARDO NAM,** actor renowned for roles in films and TV series such as *The Fast and Furious: Tokyo Drift, Sisterhood of the Traveling Pants,* and *Westworld*

"**This is a book I'll gift my nieces and nephews and other young people** as it offers tools and road maps that encourage us to trust our own creative processes and devote ourselves to a life rich with creativity, purpose, and meaning." — **AUSTIN BISNOW,** lead singer, MAGIC GIANT

THE ONE AND ONLY YOU!
How to Be the
Best, Truest, You-est You

Nicole Jon Sievers, MSW, LCSW

Contributors
Maxwell Senn, Middle School Student
Gabriel Senn, Graduate Student
Benjamin Sievers, College Student
Eric Louis Sievers, MD
Ruth Matinko-Wald, MA
Norene Gonsiewski, MSW, LCSW
Glenda Montgomery,
Teacher & Certified Positive Discipline Lead Trainer

Imaginal Discs Press
La Jolla, California

Edited by Ruth Matinko-Wald
Designed and illustrated by Darcy Cline

For information and bulk orders,
email nicolejonsievers@gmail.com.

Imaginal Discs Press
La Jolla, California

Library of Congress Control Number: 2020906778
ISBN 978-0-9964013-0-2 (paperback)
ISBN 978-0-9964013-1-9 (ebook)

Printed in the United States of America

This book is dedicated to
Maxwell Jon Daniel Senn—
whose input, insight, and humor made it possible.
It's also dedicated to my young
nieces and nephews in all your wonderful neurodiversity:
Katherine Nicole King, Maria Fox Menely, Snapper King,
Grayson Henman, and Rowan Menely.
You are all celebrated, needed, and loved.

a SPECiaL nOTE TO YOU

When I was a kid, I went through really hard stuff. I spent a lot of my youth feeling storm-tossed by the events of my life: moving, death, loss of one kind or another. I also loved the world and found a lot of magic in life.

As I got older, I realized that the magic was real and learned that some of the hardest things for me were the experiences that built my compassion, courage, and strength as an adult. Life also taught me that things didn't have to be so hard and that how I interpreted events often led me to greater pain as I blamed or rejected myself. Plus, sometimes things were just painful and nothing could change the pain; I just had to find a path forward.

I wish I'd known as a kid that no matter what, my single most important job (other than keeping myself alive and not harming others) was to be ridiculously me in all my quirky, unique, creative ways of being. Some of my most challenging experiences had me thinking I wasn't okay or good enough and that I needed to be different. Of course, evolving ourselves and growing is our job, too. But I was stuck thinking that other people had something figured out, and I was bewildered. At some point, I decided I would never be able to be what I am not and I let myself laugh more. I let myself play and come to life in a way unique to being me.

Everything I've gathered and written in this book is what I needed as a kid. It's designed to help you see you were invited to your life exactly as you are, and you are who is meant to show up. This is your most important job: to be ridiculously you among the nearly eight billion people in this world. Every single person—including you—has a different purpose, a unique story to tell, and an original life to live. With different talents, likes, and dislikes as well as different hard, blessed, or simply ordinary experiences, we all have many things to learn as well as to teach one another.

You have the potential to do something amazing with your life by being the best you. You are made of the same stuff as any of your heroes. Like them, you have an important gift, a solution to a problem, a creative force that you bring to the world—a creative force that matters just as much as the bees pollinating flowers and the sun warming the planet. You have an ordinary, extraordinary life that is uniquely yours.

So, what is YOUR genius? What is YOUR passion? What does it mean to be ridiculously YOU? Use this book to help you find out. Explore the book, skip around in it, figure out what ideas work for you and let go of those that don't. Make the book your own by circling stuff, doodling, pondering the Pause Points, and filling in your answers to questions. Write notes in the margins. Argue with me. Teach me.

Used well, *The One and Only You!* will support you in discovering and appreciating your gifts, in advancing your own masterpiece in the making. The book also will help you to make better decisions, walk a path of compassion, and discover and appreciate the gifts of others—because the problems of this world are more easily solved when we work together and the pleasures in life are more deeply enjoyed when they're shared. Onward to thriving!

Love, nicole

contents

1 first things first: own you!

You are unique. Even though you are part of a larger story, there is only one you in all of history, and you have the job of becoming the best YOU possible. The world needs your gifts! No one else can tell you what it is to be you, and who you are changes every minute. You are a masterpiece in progress. The process or journey of your creating your best self is actually your life's work. Think of that journey like a hero's quest to find the treasure of the gifts you have to create a life you love and a world that works for all.

Have you ever thought about how truly unique you are? Maybe you already know that your fingerprint is totally unique, no one else in the world looks exactly like you (even identical twins have differences), and no one has DNA in the exact sequence as you.

Did you also know your thoughts are unique to you, too? That's because you developed them based on your specific experiences. In other words, **your mind— where thoughts, feelings, and actions originate— develops through your relationships and your connections with other people and with nature.**

Everyone's experiences and relationships are different. Not even siblings have the same experiences and relationships. So, bottom line, your mind is no one else's but yours. Own it!

For a simple example, consider ice cream. What pops into your head when you read those two words? A sundae with extra fudge and cherries? Does everyone have similarly yummy thoughts? For someone who is vegan or lactose intolerant (allergic to milk products), thinking about ice cream might bring  up fears of a stomach ache or even memories of being left out—all the times they couldn't eat dessert when other kids could. Our experiences with ice cream are very different, so our thoughts, feelings, and memories about it are different, too. This is just one example, but it shows that every single person's mind works differently and that similar events can lead to very different experiences. That means no one in the world has the mind you do. That makes you entirely unique. And it means you have unique gifts to offer.

The Key of Staying Curious

For some people, uncovering their gifts and "true self" is fairly easy. They know what they like and exactly what they want to do and be, and that's great. For example, maybe some of your friends really like dogs or cats and know for sure they want to be veterinarians or vet assistants when they grow up. A few kids might be naturally good at and love gymnastics, so they are working really hard to get better and maybe compete in the Olympics someday. Most people, though, don't know what their special gifts are. Most need to keep exploring to learn more about themselves, what makes them unique, and what gifts they have to share with the world. **The key to a successful treasure hunt of the self is to stay curious.**

When you were a baby and then a toddler, being curious came really easy to you. You had everything to learn, and you wanted to know how everything worked. Ask a parent or caregiver how often you asked, "Why?" Probably a gazillion times! Now that you're older, you know a whole lot more than you did when you were little. But, guess what? You still have a lot to learn. **Now it's up to YOU to decide to stay curious, to want to learn.**

You can be curious about anything and everything. Are you curious about bees, why they are important to the survival of the human race? If so, how would you explore that? Maybe you wonder if humankind could live on Mars. Where would you go to find out if it's possible and, if not, why not, and, if so, how? Do you love music and wonder how composers put notes on a page so instrumentalists can play the same music over and over again—even for generations? What would you need to do to get to the bottom of that mystery, so you could compose music, too?

There is great power and wisdom in curiosity. Some of the happiest and most successful adults are those who stay curious and interested in the world.

your unique smarts

Understanding your unique gifts is powerful. One way to identify your gifts is to understand your "smarts." Many people underestimate their own "smarts." This is often true if you struggle with a particular subject, or maybe with school in general. It can lead you to think you are not smart. But that's just not true.

You might reconsider how you think of "smarts" and be on the lookout for areas where you shine. Maybe some school subjects come easily to you but others don't. What are those you ace? Maybe you do really well on a math test yet struggle to remember how to spell *government*. What's up with that? Maybe you're a sure-footed skier on mountain moguls but don't like to read books. What does that tell you?

According to a famous American psychologist, Howard Gardner, **there are lots of different kinds of "smarts,"** or what he called "multiple intelligences." Gardner's unique gift helped him discover that what other scientists thought of as "soft skills," such as people skills, were really types of intelligence. It makes sense. Being a math whiz might give you the ability to help the world, but so does being "people smart." Think about it: Although they might not be able to figure out all the numbers involved in building a dog house, people-smart people will be able to convince the right person to do the calculation and gather a great team together to complete the project.

See the next page for a list of the multiple smarts or intelligences Gardner identified.

Nature Smart: Being good with animals, at understanding living things, and at "reading" nature

Music Smart: Excelling at performing and composing music

Number/Logic Smart: Being good at quantifying things, making hypotheses, and proving them

Word Smart: Excelling at finding the right words to express what you mean

Picture Smart: Being good with shapes, designs, graphics, and at visualizing the world

Body Smart: Being good at performing sports, physical activities, and other body movements such as dance

People Smart: Excelling at sensing people's feelings and motives as well as being good at getting along with others and organizing groups

Self Smart: Being good at understanding yourself, what you feel, and what you want (Note: This book is helping you become more self smart!)

Pause Point When you think about all the ways of being smart, to which of them do you relate? Think about the people with whom you live. How do each of them show THEIR "smarts"? How about your best friend? Deep down inside, do you value some "smarts" more than others? If you're honest, you probably do, but ask yourself "why?" For sure it's okay that you think the way you do and value what you value! When you have a chance, though, it's always important to PAUSE and WONDER why you have certain opinions. Doing so will lead you to deeper thoughts, and deep thoughts can lead to amazing insight!

Each individual has his/her/their own combination of "smarts"—different ways of perceiving, understanding, and communicating about life experiences. Believing that any one way of knowing is better than another limits the opportuninty to create new connections and ideas. It's time to explore YOUR gifts. And how do you explore your gifts? By staying curious!

using your unique Gifts to make the world a Better Place

Things about which you are curious can help you to enjoy your life as well as figure out what unique gifts you have to contribute to improving the world. Truly, the world has lots of problems and **every individual brings something important to help solve these problems.** It's also important to know the world doesn't need just one type of "smart." To solve our problems, to create art, to live our best lives, we need all kinds and different combinations of "smarts."

Disclaimer: *While you explore and build on the areas where you shine, it's also important to work on areas where you struggle and to believe your efforts will make a difference in developing your skills.*

Great idea!

To figure out your gifts, start by asking yourself what things you are good at and what things you like: Do you rock at chess? Do you speak a different language? Are you extra funny? Can you rap or beatbox cool songs? Are you a good artist? Are you really brave? Can you do math in your head quickly? Do you try to bring joy to others? Are you a gifted athlete? Are you intuitive and feel things that others might not necessarily see or understand? Are you an adventurer? A writer? A lover of rocket ships, birds, the night sky? A thinker? Do you want to cure cancer? Clean the oceans? The world awaits your sharing who you are!

THOUGHTS & DOODLES

Think about it!

To aid you in discovering and sharing what gifts you have to offer, fill out the answers to the questions below, overflowing onto extra paper if needed. And date your answers because tomorrow they might change. We are each living artworks in progress!

If you aren't someone who likes to fill out forms, at least read through the statements and think about them. You also might share your answers and thoughts with a new friend. Doing that could help you learn more about what makes you unique.

All About Me

(date)_____

~ (Home)School ~

1. When I learn, I shine at _____

2. When I learn, I am challenged by _____

3. The things I enjoy learning most are _____
_____

4. The things I do not enjoy learning very much are _____
_____

5. When it's recess or time to take a break, I like to _____
_____

6. If I could schedule my own day of learning, it would include
_____

7. In groups, I am a leader / a follower / both. (Circle one or more.)

at Home

1. The kids in my family are older / younger / half / foster /adoptive siblings. (Circle as many as apply.)
2. My favorite thing to do at home is_____
3. My least favorite thing to do at home is _____
4. My strengths shine at home when I _____
5. I get into trouble at home when I_____
6. When I'm home, I like to play by myself / with others / with my pet / with _____(Circle one or more.)
7. When I'm sick, I feel better when _____
_____

my Hobbies

1. I feel most creative when I _____
_____
2. The music that makes me feel the most is _____
3. My favorite game is _____
4. My favorite sport is _____
5. If I could, I would watch _____ (movie) over and over.
6. I like to draw with _____
7. If I could, I would visit a library / museum / sports stadium / _____ (Circle one or more.)
8. My favorite holiday is _____
9. My favorite activity is _____
10. If I could, I would visit the mountains / seashore / desert / _____ (Circle one or more.)

food

1. My favorite food is _____

2. My least favorite food is _____

3. I like to eat healthy food / junk food / both. (Circle one or more.)

4. The one food I wish they had in the school cafeteria is _____

_____

5. If I could eat at a restaurant, I would choose _____

_____

How i Relax

1. When I want to relax, I _____

2. I relax best when I am alone / with other people. (Circle one.)

3. My favorite time to relax is before I go to bed / before I go to

school / on the weekends / _____ (Circle one or more.)

4. My favorite place to relax is _____

5. What helps me to relax is _____

friends

1. I like having only one or two / a big group of friends. (Circle one.)

2. With my friends, I'm a leader / follower / both. (Circle one or more.)

3. I like people who like the same things as I do / like different things.
(Circle one.)

4. What I admire about my friends is _____

_____

5. When my friends are with me, I hope they are feeling _____

_____

~future Plans ~

1. If I could solve a world problem, it would be _____

_____

_____

_____

_____

2. I am most curious to learn _____

_____

3. In the future, I think the world will be _____

_____

4. What I love about being me that others also appreciate is _____

_____

_____

5. What I love about being me that others don't always appreciate

is _____

Did you learn anything new about yourself? Do any of your answers surprise you? Do they help to point you toward your gifts? Write about what you learned.

_____

_____

_____

_____

_____

_____

I'm Unique! Everyone is an artist in his or her or their own way. There is room for all of us and the unique way we do things! Throughout this book, we'll suggest activities to encourage you to creatively express yourself. You can change the activities we suggest to make them your own if you'd like. Here's the first suggested activity.

What Makes ME Unique? We all come from ancestors who are unique. Your ancestors are all the people who came before you in your family: your parents, grandparents, great-grandparents, great-great-grandparents, great-great-great-grandparents . . . Whew! You get the point. All your ancestors have and had unique backgrounds and experiences. And each of them had to exist to create the YOU here today—the only one YOU in all of history. How amazing is that! Ask your friends and family members this question: "What do you think makes me unique?" Collect their answers in the clouds below. Then draw a picture of you on the next page and write their answers around your self-portrait.

 my self-portrait!

2 How Other People Can Help You Discover You

One of the best ways you learn about anything—including yourself—is by talking to and doing things with other people. Because every person has unique gifts, we all have something to learn from each other. Think about your classmates. What can you learn from them? You won't know unless you stay curious and ask them about their families, feelings, favorite activities, problems they're interested in solving, or things they like to create. Our differences can help us to see options, although we don't need to change who we are—and neither do others need to change who they are.

If you learn that a classmate is really different from you, there also is no need to be suspicious. It's actually really great! It just means your classmate lives life from a different perspective. **Perspective** is the way someone views and approaches the world. There are many ways people can view and approach the world.

Someone who uses a wheelchair looks at a staircase differently than someone who doesn't use a wheelchair. Someone who celebrates Hanukkah has different memories about the holiday season than someone who celebrates Christmas.

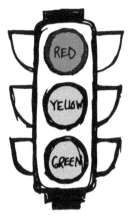

Someone who has spent many years playing baseball notices more details when watching a game than someone who has never played.

Consider this specific example to understand perspective even better: Some people are colorblind. In fact, it's possible you even have a classmate who is colorblind. Maybe it's you! People who are colorblind have trouble telling the difference between red and green. In rare cases, they cannot see color at all. Red berries on a bush might blend in. A rainbow would have fewer colors. A traffic light might have just two colors. So, if you are not colorblind, it's not anything to be afraid of, right?

But imagine how the world looks different to those who are colorblind and what they need to do to be safe and enjoy life. By "walking in their shoes" and seeing life from their perspective, you will benefit. That's because **seeing life from multiple perspectives helps YOU become a better problem solver**. And, if you're a better problem solver, then you can more easily use your gifts to make the world a better place, to have a life of more adventure, to make new friends, to become a more creative artist, to take better care of animals, to learn to respect others, or learn to feel okay or even good about who you are! Those who are "different" might find a gift in their differences, too, if you just ask about them. Even challenging differences can bring gifts. Stay curious and investigate.

Pause Point *If you could live from another person's perspective for a day, whom would you choose? What about that person awakens your curiosity? What makes you curious about how that person sees things? What would you hope to learn from that person?*

Perspective sharing

Just as people view things differently, they also share their perspective in different ways: through a simple conversation, book, song, dance, artwork, blog post, newspaper article, scientific study, YouTube video, and so much more. People are constantly being creative and finding new ways to express themselves and share their perspectives.

You have your own perspective, too. It was created by all your life experiences and by the things you think about. If you work to solve problems at school or in the world from only your perspective, however, you are not seeing the whole picture. **The best way to solve problems is with multiple perspectives.** Think about it this way: If you went to a baseball game, would you want to sit where you could only see the right field? Probably not! To be able to understand what is happening in the game, you would want to see the entire field. This is what seeing from multiple perspectives allows you to do: You can better understand what is going on! Also, think about this: In the last chapter, you learned about different "smarts." If everyone has his, her, or their own unique way of being smart, it makes sense that bringing together those multiple ways of being smart—and the multiple perspectives that it creates—will result in greater understanding. Truly, **we could tackle problems, big and small, if we could see things from all angles!**

Seeing the World from multiple Perspectives

So, how do you see from multiple perspectives? Once again, it's by being curious and by learning about and from other people. **When you can think about something from multiple perspectives, this causes your own perspective to expand.** For example, just the simple act of accepting friendship from someone different

from you can expand your perspective and enhance your life. You might make friends with someone who is Vietnamese and invites you to participate in a mid-autumn festival lantern walk. You could have a Brazilian friend who teaches you to dance samba. You might make friends who are extra creative and turn the events of their days into poems, song lyrics, or beatbox rhythms. Or you might have Muslim friends who share their delicious flatbread and teach you about their holidays and traditions.

Notice that perspectives may be reflected in food, art, music, fashion, sports, movies, and the like. That means that, by expanding your perspective, you also get to enjoy more of the beauty and creativity in our world. You get to do more, taste more, feel more, listen to more, see more, make more, learn more, and create more. You open yourself up to new, exciting experiences. This way, you get to understand more! And all these experiences provide you with more tools to explore yourself and from which to draw when you want to express yourself creatively. They enhance what makes YOU unique.

(Pause Point) So far, how are you feeling about seeing things from another's perspective? Does it feel comfortable or uncomfortable? Which one of your friends or relatives has the most different perspective from you? How would you describe the difference? Do you feel free with friends and family to share your own way of seeing things? Do you need to explore more your own way of seeing things to know your true self? There are no wrong answers!

The importance and power of Diversity

actually, every person is an individual and unique. That means every child in your class is different, so there is **diversity** in your classroom. Some diversity is obvious. Kids in your class have different skin and hair color. Some are tall and some are small. Some might walk through the door, whereas another might roll through in a wheelchair. You get the idea.

Maybe more importantly, some diversity you cannot see with your eyes. Your classmates may come from different parts of town. Some may be rich, and some may come from families who have a hard time paying bills. Some may have difficulty getting dressed in the morning because their bodies offer different challenges than yours. Still others may celebrate different holidays and eat different foods. These subtle differences you cannot immediately see might be overlooked, if you aren't curious. And then you lose out not only on making new friends but also on learning what each classmate has to teach you.

This goes for your whole life. Being curious about getting to know people can help you grow as a person, become a better problem solver, and make the world a better place. In fact, to be the best YOU possible so you can bring your gifts to the world, the success of OTHERS matters. And THEIR success and happiness can be greatly enhanced by YOU!

> i𝘯 all of nature, the greatest indicator of strength and survival is diversity.

As an example of how this works, let's say you're on a soccer team and one of your teammates hasn't played much soccer in the past. She's really numbers smart, but she isn't a very good soccer player. When she's on the field, your team doesn't do very well. On the other hand, playing soccer comes easily for you, and you know you're an asset to the team. So you have a choice: You can ignore and even make fun of this teammate who isn't very good. You can even avoid kicking the ball to her or get angry at her for her inability. Many

kids would do that, but would those approaches make your teammate or your team do better?

Instead, what you might do is offer to practice dribbling the ball with her, encourage her efforts, and help her to develop her confidence. That confidence and skill development may help her become a better soccer player, which would make your whole team better, which surely will make you happy! More importantly, that confidence might help her throughout her life. One day, she might use her math smarts to invent something that helps you or your family, or maybe she will write your favorite song. By helping her develop her confidence and skill, you contributed to her success. In a way, her success is your success, too.

See how this works? **We are all connected to one another— which also means that no one is completely alone.** But you have to get out of your room and interact with others to really feel this truth!

Another reality is that the more we support one another, the better off we all are. In other words, everyone has a gift to give, a skill to share, and a piece of the puzzle for solving the world's many problems, for **creating a world that works for all.** This is something to celebrate! Diversity is something to celebrate!

Disclaimer: *Even people you find to be negative and challenging have something to teach you. Sometimes you have to stand your ground and not allow yourself to be bullied. But, when you dig deep and respond with grace to mean behavior, you find new strength in you, learn new skills, and become an even better version of yourself.*

neurodiversity on a grand scale

Think about this idea on a grand scale. The Earth is home to close to eight billion people. That means the world has almost eight billion unique minds and nearly eight billion ways of thinking that can be used for the good of Mother Earth and humanity. This is called "neurodiversity," a word made up of the root *neuro* (having to do with the nervous system and brain) plus the word *diversity* (the state of having a wide range of different things). **Neurodiversity is one of the strengths of our species**. Different brains bring different skillsets that support our survival. And every person has a unique gift to offer to solve a problem or to create an opportunity because of the difference in perspective offered by different brains. Even differently abled brains some may call "disabled" can enrich our lives.

You have likely heard the saying, "Two heads are better than one." Now imagine eight billion heads working to improve the global and human experience, eight billion minds working to end wars, explore space, arrest and reverse climate change, save endangered species, end poverty, abolish racism, amplify kindness, advance inclusion and sustainability, and so much more. One of those eight billion minds is YOURS!

Although you have individual traits, you are shaped by your culture, race, ethnicity, environment, community, and family.

The feeling of belonging matters to each of us. "To belong'" is a hardwired desire for most living creatures. Belonging brings both opportunities and challenges. Can you think of some of both?

Think about it!

ake a few minutes to explore making new friends. Maybe even get your friends to answer the same questions. Better yet, share your answers with someone you don't know very well and ask that person the same questions. You might learn you have something in common with someone you thought was different. Many of us have a lot more in common than we know.

Have you ever been the new kid in class? If you have, consider the following questions:

➡ What did being new feel like? _____

_____

_____

➡ What was it like when someone came and talked to you when you were new?_____

_____

_____

➡ How did someone who became your friend approach you in the first place? What did that kid say or do? _____

_____

_____

_____

Have you ever struck up a friendship with someone you didn't know? It takes some courage to get to know new people, especially when they look or act differently than you do.

➡ What are some ways you can meet new people? _____

_____

_____

_____

➡ If there are no new kids at school, where might you meet someone new? _____

_____

_____

_____

➡ What are three "ice-breaker" questions you might ask to get to know someone?

1)_____

_____

_____

2)_____

_____

_____

3)_____

_____

_____

Get Creative!

● **Superpowers!** Pretend you're an investigative reporter. Ask as many people as you can (friends, family members, other kids at the bus stop . . .) what they think they're good at, what their "smarts" are, what they think their "superpower" might be. Once you have your list, write a story about how these people might work together with YOU to save the planet or the universe. You might turn your story into a comic strip with illustrations. Have fun!

and then this happened...

3 no one is perfect, But Everyone can Be creative

o you think your favorite sports pro is perfect? What about your teacher, your karate Sensei or grandmaster, or your big brother? Or is there a really smart kid in your class you think is perfect? The truth is, being perfect is impossible! There's no one perfect way to throw a football or baseball. There's no one perfect way to solve a problem. There's no one perfect way to be cool. There's no one perfect way to be a success. **No one is 100 percent perfect!** We all do best in life by living from our uniqueness—failures and flaws and all.

If you discard the idea of being perfect and, instead, pursue the higher goals of learning and sharing your unique gifts—in the classroom, on the sports field, at home, in music, and with the world—that's when YOU become boundless! That's when YOU open yourself to interesting possibilities. That's when YOU start exploring and inventing. And, that's when you will be happiest because your human brain is wired to be creative! **Being creative is one of the most rewarding expressions of the unique, once-in-a-lifetime, one-in-all-of-history YOU!** That's why you're best served to stop striving to be like a particular role model and, instead, work on being the best YOU possible.

> **perfectionism is:** *a refusal to accept any standard short of perfection— usually what you believe others think is perfection. Being good enough is good enough! Perfect to one isn't perfect to another.*

Warning: Falling into the trap of perfectionism is really easy! But it will cause you to limit yourself and not accomplish all you are capable of accomplishing with your life. Granted, paying close attention to what others have done and learning from them the skills needed to master something is important. But think about all that as a starting point. For example, when the Impressionist painters decided not to paint like the other artists of their day, they created brilliant new art. When Einstein tackled some physics problems that Newton's laws didn't address, he opened doors to new knowledge.

In other words, once you master certain skills, then it's time to start asking questions: Why this and not that? Why hasn't anyone tried such and such? What would happen if I did _____ ? What if I combined this with that? Imagine the new moto cross moves you could invent! Think about the mind-blowing music you could make! Can you even wrap your brain around the Mars living structures you could design? On the other hand, if you were trying to be perfect, you would be focusing your attention on a single, small goal that would prove that perfection. **Focusing on proving perfection kills creativity, because it limits anything new.**

Creativity *means using your unique ideas and imagination to create something. You could create an artistic work, a solution to a problem, a new sport, a novel way of looking at why people act the way they do, a support wagon for a dog that only has one back leg, a new smoothie flavor, or a million, billion, zillion other things! The possibilities are endless.*

What's it mean to Be creative?

We tend to think of being creative in artistic terms. "Creative" people write. They draw. They make music. They direct movies. They design clothes. That's all true. Being creative, however, is much more. Imagine a football coach who comes up with clever new plays that confuse the other team, enabling his team to score lots of points. Is he creative? What about a scientist who develops a new drug that wipes out a

disease? Is she creative? Or how about office workers who together figure out a process for accomplishing their projects more efficiently? Are they creative? What about someone who brings together a group of people and sets up an online signup calendar to support someone who has cancer by making meals and housecleaning? Is he creative? The answer, in all these cases, is yes! For certain!

Just like there are multiple ways to be smart, there are many ways to be creative. Creativity is also unique to you, your culture, your family, and even where you are growing up. Because so many diverse groups of people live on our planet, what might seem creative to one group is commonplace to another. In Japan, for example, many people do origami paper folding. They chat with their friends at lunch and maybe entertain their young children by folding little birds

and animals out of the restaurant menu. If you aren't familiar with origami, you might think these people are the most creative people on Earth. If you grew up folding paper into fanciful figures and shapes, you might think it's no harder than learning to add and subtract!

Pause Point *What are some of the creative talents in your family? Maybe you have an uncle who can make crazy good cakes from scratch, or maybe your mom builds beautiful furniture. Make a list of the ways you see creativity in the people around you. While you're looking around you, start to notice those things in your environment made by creative minds. Which things impress you most? Consider why you're attracted to certain things. Remember, stay curious!*

Every single one of us has the potential to be creative. **Creativity is a hallmark of being human, because our brains are designed to solve problems in service of the world's betterment.** Here's how creativity works: A problem stumps us. We think about it. And then we figure out a way around the problem because our brains are wired to care about solving the problem.

If everyone can be creative, you ask, then why doesn't everyone regularly practice that creativity? As mentioned earlier, one of the reasons is that our society—TV, movies, books, music, and more—tends to define creativity only as something "artistic." Because people see and hear this message all the time, they repeat it. If everyone is saying that "creative" means "artistic," shaking that influence is difficult, and we end up believing what we hear and see around us. That's not helpful. We need to question what we see and hear and to boldly seek the truth. And the truth is that **having a narrow definition of creativity hurts our ability to recognize and live our own originality, just as it keeps us from seeing and championing creativity in others.**

The bottom line is this: Every single person has gifts to share with the world, gifts that can make the world a better place. So, ask yourself: What is YOUR creative gift or gift of service? Are you good at tying flies for fly fishing? Have you figured out a new ice skating jump? Can you easily make people smile and laugh? Are you the calm mediator when there's trouble among your friends? Whatever your creative gift, go and use it to make magic happen! Being the best YOU is the highest form of service.

THOUGHTS & DOODLES

One thing about being creative that I'm grateful for is my ability to.....

_____
_____
_____

Think about it!

Some of us try to find accomplishment or perfection in one specific area of our life. You might try to be the star baseball player, a straight-A student, the prima ballerina, or the most well-behaved kid in class. If you are trying to be perfect in one area of your life, what area is it? How do you think being "the best" in that area will make you feel? No matter what the area, always remember it is only one area of your life. What other areas do you want to work on? What would give you joy?

Double Standards. . . . Interesting! Hmm . . . this is tough stuff! How do you feel about not trying so hard to be perfect? What do those feelings tell you about your desires to be perfect? Do you have really high standards? Do you set the bar higher for yourself than for others? Think about the following statement and see if it's true or false for you. "If my friend got a B on a test, I would be happy for her, but, if I got a B on a test, I would be really upset." This is an example of a double standard. Do you have double standards? If yes, come clean with yourself here by writing about it.

_____

_____

_____

_____

_____

_____

_____

Yippee! A Goof Up! In many areas of life, working really hard and not "getting it perfect" can teach us more than when we follow the formula exactly. In fact, it is not possible to become good at anything without failing first. **(Check this out: FAIL stands for First Attempt In Learning!)** For example, let's say you want to learn to play the clarinet. The first time you pick it up, you won't even know how to make a sound. You'll have to learn how to place your mouth and how to blow. You'll make mistake after mistake. Eventually, you will make beautiful music and find your own style, but not without first making all those mistakes, following your heart, and having fun with the instrument. To explore your experience with perfectionism, respond to the following questions:

➡ **What is one mistake you made in the area of your life where you are trying to be perfect?**

_____

_____

_____

_____

_____

_____

_____

_____

➡ **REIMAGINE IT! What came out of making that mistake that might have been positive?**

_____

_____

_____

_____

_____

_____

_____

One of Tom's Teachings: A lot of the world's most important discoveries came from people making mistakes, trying over and over, using different approaches, and not giving up. There is a story that, when trying to invent a light bulb, Thomas Edison failed over 1,000 times. His attitude was a helpful one. He is thought to have said, "I have not failed over 1,000 times. I have successfully discovered more than 1,000 ways NOT to make a light bulb." Long story short: We learn when we make mistakes.

➡️ **REIMAGINE IT! Write down your thoughts about making mistakes. How can they help you? How do you shift your feelings about having made the mistakes and move on to do things you may not have imagined possible with limited beliefs?**

_____

_____

_____

_____

_____

_____

_____

_____

_____

_____

_____

_____

_____

_____

_____

_____

_____

_____

Get Creative!

● Paper Clip Bonanza! Think about a paper clip. Grab one right now, if you can, to look at and experiment with it. What is it meant to do? Keep pieces of paper together, right? That's how you have been taught to use a paper clip. What else could it be used for? Be creative! Brainstorm as many ideas as you can in this space. Maybe draw pictures of the uses. Feel free to draw outside the lines. After thinking of ideas individually, team up with a few friends and ask them to share any ideas they have. How do your ideas change and expand as you brainstorm with others?

Uses for a Paper Clip

You might consider this activity from different perspectives!
How might a paper clip be useful to a gardener? A kid just learning math? Someone making a bird house? A mom who loses her keys all the time? By looking at the paper clip through the eyes of lots of different people, your brainstorm turns into a brain-hurricane! That's the power of exploring multiple perspectives.

Let yourself be messy.
Let yourself collide.
Let yourself clash.
Lift yourself from old
limits and into new
creative possibility.

Now, brainstorm the many ways YOU are creative.
You may surprise yourself with what a creative genius you are!

_____

_____

_____

_____

_____

_____

_____

_____

_____

_____

_____

**What's one way you once thought of yourself as "less than" and
then discovered it as a gift or creative blessing?** If this is challenging
to answer, write about it as if you're telling a friend.

_____

_____

_____

_____

_____

_____

_____

_____

_____

4 Yay, Boo, Ugh, Grrrr: understanding feelings

Let's recap where we are now: First and foremost, YOU are an amazing, unique person, and you are one in nearly eight billion people on this planet. Based on your personality and your DNA, there are many ways of expressing your intelligence and your imagination. **To come to KNOW yourself and BE yourself, you need to stay curious about yourself and the world around you and to accept your unique challenges as possibilities for positive growth.** Like everyone else, YOU have many hidden talents; you are pure potential! Always remember, however, that people who are different from you can actually help you to grow and to think more creatively. Truly, you belong to a species that can create anything imaginable!

To be your best self, you might practice being an original, creative thinker. Doing that might make you happy and excited, proud and inspired. But, putting yourself out there and trying new things and exploring might also make you scared or even embarrassed. **Feelings are important to talk about when you're discovering the treasure of yourself.**

So, what do you think about feelings—yours and those of others? What are some feelings you have a lot of the time? Are you happy, sad, excited, bored, proud, embarrassed, loving, mean, inspired, worried, grateful, scared? You might feel happy to see a friend. Mad when someone shoves you. Excited to get dessert. Upset about how much homework you have. Worried about a test. Proud you created something. Notice that some are positive or helpful feelings, and some are negative or unhelpful feelings. Both kinds of feelings—what we also call "emotions"—are important, because

every emotion teaches you something different. They help you to learn about how you think and how you see things. Emotions can teach you about some of the stories you carry in your mind about yourself, others, and the world. They even can cause you to look at something in a different way. But negative emotions sometimes lead to bad things. They can get you in trouble. They can encourage you to say or do something mean.

Emotions are powerful. Very powerful. So you need to practice self-management. Self-management is about understanding and working with your emotions to get the results you want!

Most people believe emotions come from your heart. That's not true. **Emotions really come first from your head**. They are created by your thoughts. Here's a simple explanation of how the process works:

1) An event occurs and immediately you think about that event.

2) A particular part of your brain interprets the event as helpful/unhelpful or safe/dangerous. This part of your mind can be called the "interpreter."

3) Your body then releases chemicals associated with the interpretation.

4) These chemicals enter your bloodstream and make you feel things.

5) The combination of your thoughts and feelings creates your experience of the event.

The chemical messengers in step three are called **hormones** and **neurotransmitters**. (Remember, we talked about *neuro* having to do with the nervous system and the brain? Add that idea to *transmitters*, which allow for connection, and you have chemicals that allow for certain connections in the brain and nervous system.) Some of them can be your BFFs and upbeat allies in making you feel good. Others—not so much!

Consider serotonin. This chemical is like your own personal Tinker Bell from *Peter Pan*. The story, originally by J.M. Barrie, is a classic, yet in places, unfortunately, it reinforces stereotypes that create belief systems rooted in myths, misunderstandings, and untruths. We all do better when relating to others and ourselves from a healthy place of respect! We're learning this collectively, striving to be ever more inclusive and respectful while salvaging what works from the past. Tink, for example, is a wonderful part of the *Peter Pan* story. When she sprinkles fairy dust, you just need to, "Think of the happiest things. It's the same as having wings!" In chemical terms, if you practice gratitude and think happy thoughts, your brain increases serotonin levels (like fairy dust), which basically transmits happiness throughout your whole nervous system. **So, happy thoughts make you happier!**

On the other hand, pretend you're riding your scooter near a park and a huge dog comes out of nowhere, baring its teeth at you

and barking. You think, "Oh no! I've got to get out of here. And fast!" Your body turns down the serotonin and ups the output of adrenaline and cortisol, the stress chemicals of fight and flight—and in good time, so you can escape the wrath of Rover! In short, your thoughts create and control your feelings. How cool is that?!

That nasty negativity Bias

Unfortunately, instead of being positive and proactive, people too often can get bogged down and bummed out by what others have discovered before them ("Knowing about the climate change crisis makes me sad and scared."), by what others tell them ("You can't do that!"), and by how others treat them ("Charlotte is talking about me behind my back."). Why does this happen? It's because our knowledge and experiences can make us feel bad about ourselves and others. In fact, it's really easy to notice our shortcomings, and there's a reason for that. **Our brains are programmed with a negativity bias**. That means it's easier and faster for our brains to spot what's wrong than what's right.

This negativity bias was really important to humanity's survival in our early days. We needed to be able to notice really, really fast what was off or wrong about our environment. Potential dangers and predators—cave bears, snakes, saber-toothed tigers, and even killer kangaroos and giant carnivorous lizards (really!)—lurked everywhere. **Our negativity bias is part of what protected us from being attacked, poisoned, bitten, or otherwise harmed. In current time, though, this negativity bias isn't as helpful or needed.** Instead, it causes us to have a more negative view than is real or necessary for ourselves, others, or situations. Can you see how that can make things worse for you instead of better?

Nonetheless, many of our thoughts still happen fast—like in caveperson time. Super fast! You may not even realize you had them. These speedy thoughts are called "automatic thoughts." Automatic thoughts can be helpful. For example, you probably didn't even realize you recognized Jaimee from across the cafeteria. It seemed to just happen. That's convenient, right? But some automatic thoughts cause problems by coloring an event in such a way that we become upset. For example, you could hear a sound outside your room and jump to thinking, "There must be a burglar!" which is probably not true. But the negative thought itself can still cause negative emotions such as being afraid.

We can call automatic thoughts that are negative "ANTs," for short. A for Automatic, N for Negative, and T for Thoughts! Just like the insects in your backyard (and sometimes unwelcome visitors in your house), ANTs can invade your good mood and take you down. ANTs cause negative emotions, and those negative emotions can contribute to bad decisions, poor choices, or risky behaviors. For example, an automatic negative thought could cause you to feel mad, and you might make the poor choice to hit someone. Or a different ANT might make you feel so anxious you avoid going to a party when you could have had fun. ANTs also can cause you not to give certain people a chance. A particular automatic negative thought might cause you to judge, ignore, or even make fun of someone—even if that person was really nice and you could have become great friends. In these cases, you need ANT control!

Just like supervillains, however, ANTs are often in disguise and hard to spot. You might even confuse ANTs with difficult emotions. They're different. Whereas ANTs can lead you down the wrong path—to negative thinking and behavior—you need ALL your feelings. If you're in real danger or trouble, for instance, you'll rightly be scared so you can be careful and get away or tell a responsible adult. If you lose something or someone important to you, you'll rightly be sad, mourn, and maybe even cry. Plus, without anger, Martin Luther King Jr. would have done nothing and Rosa Parks would never have sat down on the bus. **ALL feelings are valid and important. It's the ANTs we need to watch out for!**

Typical Types of ants

Because they are so common, certain categories of ANTs can easily be spotted. Think about the following examples of automatic negative thoughts and how often they creep into your life or you see someone else dealing with them.

Mind-Reading ANTs
Believing you know what others are thinking or why they are doing something without having accurate or enough information

> **Healthy Balanced Thinking:**
> *"I'm curious about that. Please tell me more."*

You know you're not a mind reader, but this common ANT will make your think you are! For example, a new girl comes to school. You try to introduce yourself, but she walks away. Mind-Reading ANTs would have you believe you know exactly what the girl was thinking—that she didn't like you! But how would you know that? You can't read minds! Sure, some people have strong intuition, the gift of understanding something without direct information, but be careful not to confuse that with knowing really what's running through someone else's brain. There could be a million other reasons why the new girl walked away: Maybe she didn't hear you. Maybe she is really shy and got scared. Without checking for accuracy, for what's REAL, you can believe your negative conclusions and your brain will convince you to give up on people and things before you give them a chance.

Granted, intuition, or having a "gut feeling" about something or someone, can be a powerful strength. For intuition to be useful, however, we must protect it from Mind-Reading ANT. We do that by pausing, assessing our thoughts for negativity bias, being curious about the facts, and making decisions based on reality.

Taking-Things-Too-Personally ANTs

Believing you are the target or the cause of every negative thing

> **Healthy Balanced Thinking:**
> *"What others think and do is mostly about them. I live by my values and can't control how others think or respond. I can only manage myself."*

When you walk down the hall at school, do you think other kids are laughing at you? When you went to see your favorite team in person and they lost, did you automatically think you jinxed them? How about when your friend's dad, who'd never been in a crash, wrecked his car while driving you to practice? Did you think you made that happen? Unless you're secretly a Harry Potter-like wizard who's been cursed by an evil magician, probably not. In fact, you probably never even entered into the minds of any of those people or had any effect whatsoever on any of the events. The kids laughing? One of them might have told a joke he heard on *Saturday Night Live* right before you came down the hall. Your favorite team probably lost because a bunch of their players were hurt. And your friend's dad? Sometimes accidents just happen, and the law of averages says he was bound to get into a crash at some point.

But if Taking-Things-Too-Personally ANTs are in control, you immediately assume that everything happening around you is because of you. It makes you take every little thing personally—from the kid "trying" to annoy you by tapping his pencil to your class losing out on a pizza party because you didn't get an A on a test (never mind the other kids who also didn't get As). When you find yourself stuck in this ANT hill, take a step back and ask yourself if your thoughts really make sense or if there's another explanation. In reality, not everything is always about YOU. If that's the way you think, Taking-Things-Too-Personally ANTs are running your life and you need to get those pesky ANTs under control.

Labeling ANTs

Judging people, including yourself, and putting others into negative categories

---

Healthy Balanced Thinking:
"I'm curious why I'm applying this label to this person (when I don't really know him/her/them). What does the label really mean? (Often, not much at all.) Who really is this person? (A whole lot more than a label.)"

Can you tell if you're going to like—or dislike—someone at a glance? If you said yes, then you've fallen victim to Labeling ANTs. Balanced, rational thoughts would tell you that people's external appearances have nothing to do with who they are on the inside are or what they are capable of. But Labeling ANTs try to get you to ignore those rational thoughts and judge people based on an immediate, automatic reaction to their clothes, eye shape, color of their skin, or the like. And then you put a label on a particular person. For example, you think because a girl in your class has blue hair that she's a rebel. In truth, she might just like the color blue and be as kind and considerate as can be. Plus, rebels can be kind and considerate! **Labeling never gets to the essence of any person.**

Labeling ANTs also have another trick that's just as nasty: **They can make you label yourself.** "Oh, I can't do that, because I'm not a creative person." "I'll fail that test, because I'm so dumb." "I'm a loser, so no one will hang out with me." Not a creative person. Dumb. A loser. These are just a few examples of false labels you can give yourself with the help of Labeling ANTs. Start to believe these labels and they can limit what you believe and what you try and accomplish. They can hide the truth about who you are. And they can hurt your character and make you feel really bad about yourself. On the other hand, **balanced, realistic thinking can stop Labeling ANTs in their tracks.**

All-or-Nothing ANTs

Believing there's only one way to think about things, only one answer to questions, only one solution to problems

Healthy Balanced Thinking:
"Many things can be true at once."

Do you like pizza or hot dogs? Math or English? Rowan or Maxwell? Can't you like them all? Not according to All-or-Nothing ANTs.

These ANTs make you choose one option and completely diss the other. There's no gray area. No choice in-between. And no room for mistakes or imperfection. Either you are a loser or cool. Either your friends are attractive or ugly. Either a situation is good or bad. Fortunately, real life isn't so black-and-white. Instead, **reality is sticky and messy and colorful and imperfect and wide ranging in its spectrums of everything.** In fact, a secret in this life and a really healthy thing to know is that **many things can be true at the same time. Even opposites can be true at once!** So, how do you deal with All-or-Nothing ANTs? Call them what they are—narrow, biased thinking—be grateful for reality, and embrace the fullness of life!

Blowing-Things-Up ANTs

Making a really big deal out of something small, or making something a little negative seem like the worst thing ever

Healthy Balanced Thinking:
"This, too, shall pass."

Have you ever felt like your life is over? That you ruined everything? Well, you can thank Blowing-Things-Up ANTs for those feelings. The talent of this category of ANTs is making you feel like a small misstep is actually a giant catastrophe, because Blowing-Things-Up ANTs specialize in exaggerating the negative.

Here's usually how Blowing-Things-Up ANTs work: Let's say you spilled some paint on your shirt while you were making a birdhouse. You think your shirt is completely ruined and that you'll never be able to wear it again. On top of that, your mom is going to go ballistic when she sees it. She might yell at you, ground you, and keep you from going to your friend's birthday party over the weekend.

Then you'll never have any friends and no joy forever! Seriously?! Over some paint on your shirt? Good problem solving and balanced thinking can bring you to another reality. The reality is you could probably wash out the paint from your shirt and tell your mom that you are sorry about the spilled paint, that you'll be more careful in the future. Maybe she will be so excited about your being creative that she won't be upset at all!

If you find yourself exaggerating how bad something is, take a moment to think through the circumstance. Are the consequences you're imagining realistic? Or are Blowing-Things-Up ANTs helping you to blow the consequences out of proportion? In reality, life is full of goof-ups, big and small. **There's no need to turn everything into a horrible catastrophe.**

Ignoring-the-Good ANTs

Ignoring or downplaying anything positive

> **Healthy Balanced Thinking:**
> *"In this moment, this feels good."*

Whereas Blowing-Things-Up ANTs turn everything into a catastrophe, Ignoring-the-Good ANTs downplay anything positive. When you're complimented, these ANTs cause you to find some reason to disagree and lessen your value. When good things happen, you discount them as one-offs, something weird and out of the ordinary.

Something important to know about Ignoring-the-Good ANTs is that they can cause people to bully others. They prey on the fact that all people sometimes struggle with feeling bad about themselves and wonder if they are "worth" anything. This causes some people to bully others because deep down inside they don't think they are worth much and want to "steal" worth from another. Others bully because they  think, "I'm worth more than others, so I can dump my frustrations on anyone I choose!" But here's the truth about worth: We are all born with one unit of worth. Everyone—no matter how rich or poor, how educated or not, which country we're born in, which religion we belong to, what color our skin is, whether we

 are big or small, old or young, a rock star or homeless—**EVERYONE has one giant unit of worth! No one can steal or buy yours or take it away. You can't steal anyone else's either. Your worth is a like a golden coin in your heart.** Polish it, feel it, and remember: It's yours alone.

But Ignoring-the-Good ANTs try to tell you differently! That A+ you got in Math last week? A fluke! The test must have been easier than usual. That compliment your coach gave you? She was just trying to be nice. The award you got in art? Who cares? It was just a small award. Nothing important. Ignoring-the-Good ANTs always help you to find a way to disagree, lessen, or devalue anything good or positive that comes your way. These ANTs are trying to make you doubt your own worth, or the worth of others. Don't fall for them!

YOU *can never gain or lose your worth. It just is because you are.*

Jumping-to-Conclusions ANTs

Thinking you know what will happen in the future and that it will be dangerous or disastrous

> **Healthy Balanced Thinking:**
> *"Things are not often what they seem. Something that seems like a rejection might lead me to a better place. I stay open to this possibility."*

You just know your teacher is going to call on you. And those kids who've been glaring at you? They're going to try to steal your new sneakers. But the real kicker is the school talent show this weekend, when you are definitely going to crash and burn. Can you guess what Jumping-to-Conclusions ANTs do? Yep! They jump to the conclusion that the future (whether it's an event or your whole life) is going to be dangerous or disastrous. Why? Just because! So, you end up being really stressed out all the time.

Think about it, though: You can't know how something is going to turn out until it actually happens! It's kind of like how meteorologists can't always precisely predict the weather. They might say it's going to be sunny, but as soon as you get to the park it storms. The point is, just like in every time travel movie you've ever seen, the future isn't set. There's no predicting it with 100 percent accuracy. You might be right that things will be horrible, or they could turn out perfectly fine. Unfortunately, though, **once you see a situation as disastrous or dangerous, your body follows along, sending out feelings as though the disaster has already struck.** Remember we talked about our body's chemical "neurotransmitters" earlier? That's why you need to stop this ANT in its tracks. If you don't, you can end up in full-blown panic mode.

Shoulda-Coulda-Woulda ANTs
Believing things have to be a certain way

> **Healthy Balanced Thinking:**
> *"I might not always get the result I want, but it will all work out okay."*

D istant cousins of Jumping-to-Conclusions ANTs are Shoulda-Coulda-Woulda ANTs. Instead of panicking about the future, though, Shoulda-Coulda-Woulda ANTs make you live in the past by causing you to second guess every single thing you do: "Shoot! I should have answered C instead of B." "Why didn't I take Chorus instead of Art?" "I could have gone to Sarah's party. I bet it's way more fun than John's sleepover."

THE PUNISHER

Life is made up of what happens. Some of it is earned, but much of it is just random. There will always be other, different choices you could have made. But constantly beating yourself up about the decisions you make doesn't fix anything. All it does is make you feel guilty, sad, angry, or depressed. What a waste of energy, time, and talent! The key to dealing with these ANTs is planning. **Planning gives you the power that ruminating ("shoulda-coulda-woulda") takes away.**

Pause Point Let's recap and think about the different kinds of ANTs:

Mind-Reading	Taking-Things-Too-Personally
Labeling	All-or-Nothing
Blowing-Things-Up	Ignoring-the-Good
Jumping-to-Conclusions	Shoulda-Coulda-Woulda

Circle those you use most. Can you recall a time your "interpreter" misread a situation and caused you to overreact unnecessarily? What do you think might happen if you called out an ANT for the downward negative spiral it causes?

Take Off Those Dark-colored Glasses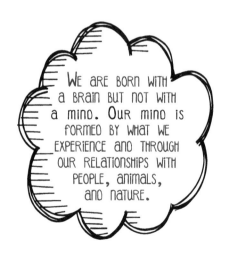

Getting hung up in an ANT hill, or in negativity bias, is like wearing the opposite of rose-colored glasses. You have on dark-colored glasses making it harder for you to see your many amazing gifts. Imagine you get your report card and see five As and one C. What are you likely to focus on? With those dark-colored glasses, probably that C, even though it's a passing grade! Disappointing, huh? But try taking off the dark-colored glasses. That C grade is only one grade on your report card; you got all As otherwise. You rock! What's important is to consider why you did so well in the other subjects but not the one. If you investigate and figure out where you do well, you may be able to use that information to bring up that C grade, too. Maybe you learned a lot even if it isn't recognizable by a good grade.

When you only look at the negative, you tend to overlook the ways you are achieving. This can prevent you from fully using your many gifts. Sometimes it can cause you to make choices that take you off the path from being your best self. But there's good news: **You have the ability to change your habits and create new ways of thinking, thanks to "neuroplasticity."**

Your "Plastic" Brain

Your brain isn't really made of plastic, but it can be "molded" just like plastic. Because of its neuroplasticity, your brain has the potential to change and adapt to new experiences. Imagine that!

How does this adapting work? Every baby is born with brain cells called "neurons." As we take in information from the world, our brain starts making

We are born with a brain but not with a mind. Our mind is formed by what we experience and through our relationships with people, animals, and nature.

connections between those neurons. These connections are called "neural pathways." Each neuron can make many connections to other neurons. These happen through experiences and interactions. The more we use a particular pathway, the stronger it becomes. It's sort of like an unmarked trail in a forest, the kind of trail that wasn't put there on purpose. Instead, it was created because so many people or animals walked along that particular path. The more it is used, the more noticeable the trail became. If people or animals stopped using that pathway, however, it would eventually fill up with grass and weeds. It wouldn't be as noticeable anymore.

Your brain's neural pathways are similar. The more you use a particular pathway, the stronger it becomes. This is why practicing a particular skill makes you better at that skill. Every time you practice, you strengthen certain connections between neurons. You are "walking" on the neural pathway, making it stronger, making it easier for you to do that specific thing. On the other hand, if you don't engage in a particular skill as often, then the pathway can become weak. The grass and weeds start growing back, blocking the way. Makes sense, right? Well, guess what? This is also true for what you think and feel. **When you think something, it is more likely you will think it again. When you feel something, it is more likely you'll feel it again.**

The Power of Positive Thinking

That means, if you practice thinking positive thoughts and having positive feelings, then those types of thoughts and feelings will more likely happen again. Yep, you can actually change your brain to change your mind to be more likely to think and feel positively. In other words, you can exterminate your ANTs! Once you do, bingo! You better control and manage your emotions! Just remember, though, that it's okay to sometimes let yourself feel unpleasant things. If your pet rat dies, for instance, you're going to feel sad. That's healthy and normal. You just don't want to get stuck

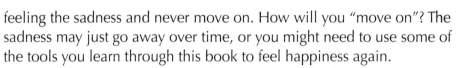

Understanding *and directing your thoughts and not letting your "interpreter" cause unnecessary upsets will help you to grow wiser. Wisdom means having knowledge and good judgment. It is something we build through lots of experience watching our thoughts and learning how to not let ANTs affect our actions — and through listening to and learning from the thoughts and experiences of others.*

feeling the sadness and never move on. How will you "move on"? The sadness may just go away over time, or you might need to use some of the tools you learn through this book to feel happiness again.

In order to manage your ANTS, you need to know your ANTs are unique to you. Although all people have some ANTs in common, no two people have exactly the same ANTs. This is because no two people have the exact interpretation of an experience. Remember, it's your interpretation of an event or experience that determines how your mood will be affected.

Because events and experiences trigger thoughts in the first place, **one powerful way to influence your ANTs is by having more corrective positive experiences.** Let's say you fear spiders. They just give you the heebie-jeebies. Every time you see one, even if just in a photo, an ANT pops up in your brain that tells you the spider is dangerous—even if it isn't. Now, what if you allowed yourself to have different experiences with spiders? Get creative. Get silly. Maybe you put plastic spiders in your ice cubes, get a stuffed animal of a spider and give it a crazy name, draw pictures of really cute, happy spiders, or listen to the "Itsy, Bitsy Spider" song over and over again. Anything goes! You might even really challenge yourself by petting or holding a spider at your local zoo or pet shop. It will be hard at first, but once you do it, you will realize it's not a big deal.

Eventually, after all your positive spider experiences, when you see a spider, your brain will click into your cute spider drawings, your cuddly stuffed spider, playfully singing "Itsy, Bitsy Spider," or the fuzzy spider you were brave enough to touch. You will have corrected your old judgments of spiders and allowed yourself to have a positive experience to remember forever. You would have widened your narrow view of spiders and replaced your ANTs with realistic thoughts! Having those realistic, calm thoughts means you now have more control over your negative emotions. When you learn how to control your emotions, you'll feel like you have a super power. You will feel like a super YOU!

Yes, Manage Your Emotions . . . but allow Them!

This entire chapter has been about *managing* your emotions and how important doing so is. *Allowing* them is equally as important! The key is to acknowledge emotions without making them bigger than they are, and then to do what needs to be done to keep you and others safe. Sometimes we need sad, mad, and scared feelings. They all can belong!

One popular tool for dealing with difficult emotions is called RAIN. It was developed over twenty years ago by a meditation teacher named Michele McDonald. The acronym RAIN stands for **Recognize**, **Allow**, **Investigate**, and **Non-Identification**. More recently, "N" is referred to as **Nurture**, which is how we use it here in this simple RAIN practice:

Recognize your feeling. Give the feeling a name if you can. Identifying the feeling can take away its power.

Allow the feeling to be just as it is. It may be unpleasant, but know it will pass.

Investigate the feeling with kindness. How does it feel in your body? What types of thoughts does the emotion cause? Approach it with curiosity.

Nurture yourself. This emotion is not who you are; it's just a feeling that will go away with time.

The idea of "RAIN" is to learn to notice our emotions with kindness before we act on them. For more on this practice and other mindfulness tools to help in dealing with difficult emotions, see blissfulkids.com.

Your Brain:
Operations
Central

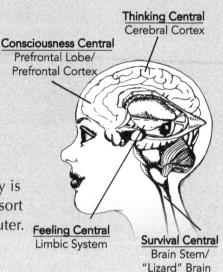

Thinking Central
Cerebral Cortex

Consciousness Central
Prefrontal Lobe/
Prefrontal Cortex

Feeling Central
Limbic System

Survival Central
Brain Stem/
"Lizard" Brain

The human brain evolved over a long period of time. Although it doesn't always operate perfectly, it's an incredibly amazing and complex organ that basically is our main operating system, sort of like the inside of a computer. It controls pretty much everything about you.

As we explore ideas throughout this book, it'll be helpful to know how different brain parts are involved in what we think, feel, and do. To start, let's go over some general information that's CURRENTLY known about the brain. (Isn't it exciting that in YOUR lifetime, new research will further brain science?) We'll begin with an overview of the four main sub-systems of the brain, what some researchers call **Survival Central, Feeling Central, Thinking Central,** and **Consciousness Central**. When all is going well, these sub-systems work together in harmony. But humans shouldn't kid themselves; it's Survival Central, the part of the brain that's the remnant of our reptile ancestors, that's usually in charge.

Survival Central is our brain stem. It's the brain part shared by all animals from reptiles to humans and often is referred to as our "lizard" brain. This part of the brain keeps us breathing and safe. Because it needed to keep humans alive in a really scary world early in our evolutionary history, it makes sense that the lizard brain reacts ridiculously fast—otherwise we would not exist because our ancestors would have been eaten by saber-toothed tigers or some other predator![1]

As humans evolved, we added a "mammalian brain" that's officially known as the limbic system or **Feeling Central.** It's in charge of releasing powerful chemicals that create feelings and sensations. It also stores those emotions so the brain can return to them for comparisons of various situations, even without our realizing our brain is doing this work. In short, the limbic system combines higher thinking with primitive emotion. Because of it, mammals such as humans have the ability to react to danger through flight, fighting, freezing, or appeasing.[2]

The third brain sub-system is called **Thinking Central** and consists of the highly evolved cerebral cortex. This area can send messages to the limbic system and is where our ability to communicate and even self-talk takes place. It's also wired with different kinds of memories, some we cannot consciously remember and others that have time and context which impact how we feel and behave.[3]

Finally, **Consciousness Central** comprises the frontal lobe, home to the prefrontal cortex—the part of the human brain that is bigger than that of every other species on the planet. It's the region that controls judgment and planning; it allows you to override messages sent by your emotions (the limbic system) so you make wiser choices. In fact, it's the only part of your brain that can witness what you are doing, answer the question of why you are doing something, and check in to see if what you are thinking and feeling is accurate, logical, and productive. What's extra interesting about this part of your brain is that it's still developing in you—and won't be completely developed until you're in your twenties. You truly are a work in progress![4]

So, the next time you feel scared or worried or anxious, think about how your brain works. Maybe you will be able to control your ANTs and prevent your limbic system from mis-interpreting the experience and going into survival mode!

How Do Your ANTs Limit You?

Review the descriptions of common categories of automatic negative thoughts (ANTs) listed in this chapter and reflect on which ones get in the way of your living your fullest life. Do you tend to blow things up, take things too personally, or label others? Do you think there's only your way or the highway? Are you always second-guessing yourself? First circle the particular ANTs that tend to creep into your life and then write about how they limit you.

ANTs	How They Limit Me
Mind-Reading	
Taking-Things-Too-Personally	
Labeling	
All-or-Nothing	
Blowing-Things-Up	
Ignoring-the-Good	
Jumping-to-Conclusions	
Shoulda-Coulda-Woulda	

YOU ARE WORKING TOWARD NEW POSSIBILITIES
AND MORE EASE IN YOURSELF. IT IS A GIFT TO YOURSELF
TO BE COMFORTABLE IN YOUR OWN SKIN.

Pay attention to your emotions for one day.
(Start with one day and it will become many!)

The label (word) we associate with each emotion begins as a physical feeling. Most people skip through the experience in their bodies and go straight to labeling the emotion with a word or acting out in a way in reaction to the emotion they feel without being aware of its sensation. In other words, many people are at a loss about how each emotion feels.

When you are paying close attention to your emotions today, be really open to discovering how each emotion is experienced uniquely by YOU. Write down details about what your body feels before you label that emotion. Explain it in words and draw it. For example, when you feel angry, where in your body do you feel it? What is the sensation like? Does it feel like waves? Does it feel like swarming bees? What color does it feel? Use the body outline on the page here to draw your emotions in the colors and patterns and places you feel them. This is creating a map to YOU!

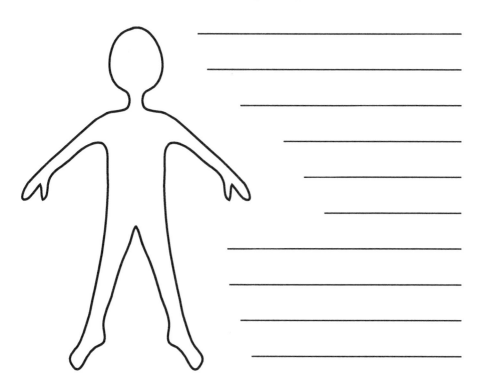

Emotion Art! Here's a fun challenge for you. Take one of the emotions you felt, described, and drew in the last activity and really explore it in a bigger and deeper way. Focus on only one of the emotions. Use a full page to draw it or paint it. Or, if you are drawn to music, think deeply about that particular emotion and create a wordless song that portrays it. If you feel like moving, find a space to dance it or act it out. Another option would be to find things in the real world that seem to portray that emotion and photograph them. *The sky's the limit!*

Happiness Brain Chemicals: How You Can Create Them!

Dopamine: **Feel Good**
Do and complete stuff
Eat something yummy
Get enough sleep
Make or listen to music

Serotonin: **Mood**
Exercise
Meditate
Sit in the sun
Remember happy events

Oxytocin: **Love**
Hug
Talk to someone you
care about
Give compliments
Enjoy your pet(s)

Endorphins: **Pain Killers**
Laugh, laugh, laugh
Exercise
Smell good things like
vanilla or lavender
Eat dark chocolate

One Sure way to lift your mood is **AN ATTITUDE OF GRATITUDE.** What are you grateful for?

_____

_____

5 Take That, ANTS!

Every thought you have comes from somewhere. You learned to have every single thought in your brain. This doesn't mean your thoughts aren't original or creative. In fact, they're completely unique. But what makes them unique isn't the fact that you create them out of thin air. The reason every single person's thoughts are unique and original is because no one has the exact same experiences.

We all learn every day—even when we are not in school. **We learn from everything that happens to us, everything around us, and everyone in our life.** We learn from TV, movies, books, and the Internet. We learn from animals, plants, and art projects. Most importantly, we learn from our family, friends, and classmates. We also belong to a culture. Actually, most people belong to many cultures! A culture is the way of life of a certain group of people. And most of us belong to many different groups. Think of all the groups you belong to: You belong to a racial or ethnic group. You belong to a group of people born in a specific country. (This is called your nationality.) You might belong to a religious group or a club with others who hold the same interests as you. The truth is that you have a unique collection of cultures. It is part of what makes you beautifully different. Each of these cultures teaches you certain beliefs and behaviors.

Our individual uniqueness and creativity comes from how our brain takes in all these various learning sources, absorbs messages we receive, and interprets those messages. Think about it this way: If you have a sibling, you're probably learning similar things and having similar experiences (although no two people ever have exactly the same experiences). Every thought you both have comes from these things you learn, BUT you and your sibling don't feel the same way about everything, right? In fact, your siblings might be so different there are times you wonder if you're really related. The reason is because **each of you takes in and interprets the information in different ways. And what comes out is unique to each of you!** One of you may accept all the rules and ideas your parents or caregivers pass on to you, and the other may be a total rebel. It's like we all have our own personal interpreter.

WE NEED OUR REBELS! Many of the most positive human rights changes have come from rebels.

Lessons: Positive and negative

Many of the lessons you learn from your experiences, other people, the media, and cultures are positive ones. They can teach you about the world. They can keep you safe. They can show you how to be good to others. They can make you the unique person you are. They can help you to become your best self.

For example, you stay up late one night. The next day, you have trouble in school. You cannot focus. Your mom says it's because you did not get enough sleep. Your experience and your mother both taught you a lesson: Sleep is important. This is a positive lesson. It created a true, realistic thought.

But we learn negative lessons, too. These lessons can be untrue. They may be unhelpful. They may lead you to make poor decisions. These lessons make it harder to become your best self. Think about giving a class presentation when you forgot everything you were supposed to say. The next time you give a presentation, a voice in your head  says you will fail again. Why? You failed once. But that does not mean you will fail again! The next time you prepare more. You use flashcards. But you believe the voice, and it makes you feel nervous. That voice taught you a negative lesson. It created automatic negative thoughts that catastrophize. Remember the Blowing-Things -Up ANTs in the last chapter. Those ANTs are not true thoughts. They are not realistic. Unless you realize that, though, Blowing-Things-Up ANTs lead to negative feelings. But you CAN control the ANTs! You just have to teach yourself a new way to think.

> Different behaviors get you different results.

Get REaL!

How can you learn a new way to think? It takes intention and practice. In other words, you have to try hard to do this. One key way is to replace your automatic negative thoughts with realistic thoughts. So, **learn to "Get REAL" with yourself!** Here is an example of how to do this:

Your teacher asks a question. You think you know the answer, so you raise your hand. It turns out your answer is wrong. That makes you feel embarrassed and a little angry. Two follow-up scenarios are possible as you sit in class the following day:

If Jumping-to-Conclusions ANTs are in Control:
You think, "I really hope I don't get called on. I just know I'll get the question wrong again." So you duck your head to make it harder for your teacher to see you. Your hands sweat. You feel awful.

If you Get REAL:
You think, "It did not feel good to get the answer wrong yesterday, but that doesn't mean I'll get it wrong today. In fact, there's a good chance I'll get it right. I did the homework this time and studied." So you sit up straight. You pay attention. If you think you know the answer to a question, you raise your hand and answer.

Which response seems healthier? Which one makes you feel better? Yep, the "Get REAL" one! You changed your behavior by studying and got a different and positive outcome. Good for you! See how you are in charge here?

anT Radar: your values

One great way to spot an ANT is to see if it goes against your values. What are values? They are the important beliefs you live by. **Your**

values help you to define what is "helpful" and "not helpful." Values help you to do what you believe is positive and healthy. They keep you from doing what you think is negative or hurtful. You get to define your values. No one else can. For example, maybe you believe it's really important to try your hardest at whatever you do. In other words, you value determination and hard work. But there's a time you just can't hit the ball during a baseball game—and Labeling ANTs show up with negative, destructive thoughts of "I'm such a loser! I should quit the team!" If, instead, you remember that you always try your hardest, you can control those ANTs and be honest about the fact that all ballplayers have a bad day now and again.

Something else to remember is that, if you feel like your values make you "weird," remind yourself that every single person around you is weird, too, because each person is unique! And that's a good thing, because all our weirdness is what helps human beings as a group to grow, to learn new things, to evolve, to be creative, to solve problems, and more. Here are a few examples of common values:

acceptance	Hard work	peace
community	Humor	self-compassion
creativity	kindness	self-love
determination	knowledge	service
fairness	Leadership	silliness
family	Loving animals	success
friendship	Loving the earth	Truth
fun	Loving others	wisdom

Sometimes you may find yourself doing something that goes against your values. When that happens, ask yourself why. **Poor choices and actions often start with ANTs!** If you know what you value, it is easier to see when ANTs lead you to act against them. This can help you to be the person you want to be.

How your Brain Works
overcoming the Lizard in Charge

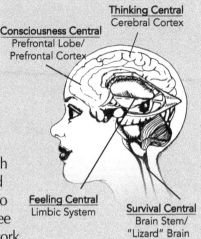

Thinking Central
Cerebral Cortex

Consciousness Central
Prefrontal Lobe/
Prefrontal Cortex

Feeling Central
Limbic System

Survival Central
Brain Stem/
"Lizard" Brain

When you see or hear something scary, **Survival Central** (the "lizard brain") and **Feeling Central** (the limbic system) can kick in and quickly flood your blood stream with stress chemicals such as cortisol and adrenaline. These might cause you to run or freeze in place. If what you see or hear makes you mad, they can work together and release those same chemicals and trigger you to fight. As we learned in the last chapter, a big job of the limbic system is to protect you from danger by working along with the primitive brain.[5]

But, beware! Your limbic system can overreact. This happens if an automatic negative thought causes the limbic system to see something as dangerous that really isn't. That's why it's so important to control your ANTs! Maybe, for instance, you see a girl wearing a special type of scarf around her head called a "hajib" and you automatically think the negative thought that she's scary (Labeling ANTs). Your danger-phobic limbic system would cause you to avoid her. If, instead, you could control your Labeling ANTs, then your danger-phobic limbic system would not overreact and you would realize that girl is human just like you and could possibly be a really good friend.

The way you override mis-interpretations by the limbic system is by engaging the higher functioning parts of your brain: **Thinking Central** (cerebral cortex) and **Consciousness Central** (frontal lobe/ prefrontal cortex). You do this by taking a deep breath, calming down, and paying attention to or "witnessing" what's really going on. The breathing and calming down is important, because, when you have less blood in an area of your brain, the less ability there is to utilize that area of the brain. Breathing and calming down allows blood to flow into your cerebral cortex and frontal lobe instead of having all your blood flowing into the most primitive parts of your brain.

THOUGHTS & DOODLES

Happy people
tend to be
grateful people.

Think about it!

Reinforcing Realistic Thoughts

In your own words, answer the following questions and give an example of each.

➡ **What is an automatic negative thought?**

_____
_____
_____
_____
_____
_____
_____
_____

➡ **What is a realistic thought?**

_____
_____
_____
_____
_____
_____
_____
_____

Reinforcing Your Values

Make a list of some of YOUR values.

---------------------   ---------------------   ---------------------
---------------------   ---------------------   ---------------------
---------------------   ---------------------   ---------------------
---------------------   ---------------------   ---------------------
---------------------   ---------------------   ---------------------
---------------------   ---------------------   ---------------------
---------------------   ---------------------   ---------------------
---------------------   ---------------------   ---------------------

Now, think about a time you were very proud of yourself. Describe that time in the space below. Why were you proud? Then, look at your list of values. Which of the values on your list were ones you feel "matched" when you were so proud of yourself? You might circle them.

When you are proud of yourself, consider that it's often because you are living out your values! How might understanding that help you? What other values do you have that are important to you? You might add to your list.

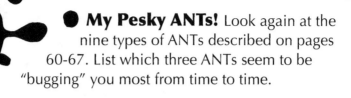

My Pesky ANTs! Look again at the nine types of ANTs described on pages 60-67. List which three ANTs seem to be "bugging" you most from time to time.

#1 _____

#2 _____

#3 _____

If ANTs really were insects, what do you think they would look like? Would they be big or small? What color would they be? How many legs would they have? Consider the three ANTs you noted as bugging you the most and draw each of them with the unique look each might have.

6 sometimes "Being Green" isn't Easy

One common cause of ANTs is feeling different. When you feel different, you may tell yourself something's wrong with you. Others may tell you this, too. It's important to know that's not true. In fact, our **strength comes from being different!**

Have you ever watched the Disney classic *Dumbo,* which is based on a story by Helen Aberson and Harold Pearl? In the movie, a circus elephant is born with huge ears and given a mean nickname: Dumbo. Everyone tells Dumbo to be ashamed of his big ears. They laugh at, make fun of, and bully him, so Dumbo feels bad about himself. In a nutshell, life isn't easy for the little elephant. One day, however, Dumbo's friend Timothy the Mouse tells him something powerful: "The very things that hold you down are going to lift you up." Eventually, Dumbo learns that his gigantic ears allow him to fly, and he becomes the star of the show!

What made Dumbo different was his greatest strength. That could be true for you, too. You just may be able to conquer problems of the world with your uniqueness! People may tell you otherwise. You might tell yourself otherwise at times, too. Never doubt, though: Just like Dumbo found where he could shine, you, too, will find a place to shine with all your differences and specialness. That place might not be clear now, so **it's important to be strong in the face of challenges. That's called being resilient.**

Imagine if Dumbo had not kept searching for his place in the world: He would never have defied the laws of gravity and discovered

Racism is ugly. Stay beautiful!

> **Resilience** *is being strong in the face of challenges. It doesn't mean you can't stumble or fall. It just means you get back up and try again or choose a different path. The point is you keep walking even if it's in a different direction.*

something so unique and beautiful about himself—that he could fly. So don't be afraid to embrace what makes YOU different! And tell those Labeling ANTs and Ignoring-the-Good ANTs to get out of town, or rework them into something life-affirming and helpful!

Note: Because of the bullying and other stereotypical, negative depictions throughout the movie, Disney Plus pulled *Dumbo* from children's profiles. It's important to know, though, that many things can be true at the same time. A book or film, like *Dumbo*, can offer positive messages and gifts, while simultaneously reinforcing stereotypes, messages, and images that culturally we have wised up to no longer accept as true, fair, or healthy. There's a saying, "Forgive yourself for what you do not know—until you know it—and then DO BETTER!"

sometimes "Being Green" isn't Easy

Let's consider another example. Jim Henson's Muppet character Kermit the Frog sings a song called, "It's Not That Easy Bein' Green." In the song, Kermit shares his feelings about not being like everyone else and just being himself. Like with Kermit, you might find that sometimes it's not easy being who you are. Sadly, kids tease and make fun of each other for wearing certain clothes, having a particular birthmark, being a different skin color, wearing glasses, learning differently, and tons of other things. Teasing and taunting can really hurt. You may even want to throw an insult back or want to run and hide. No one likes to be hurt and feel bad. In situations like this, you should remember two things:

> **patience** *is being able to accept delay, the unknown, excitement, trouble, or suffering without getting mad or upset. That's hard sometimes! Being patient with yourself and others also can help you to RESPOND instead of REACT. Self-management is power!*

First, the words and actions of others say more about them than about you. They may be lashing out at you because they feel uncomfortable about what makes them different or because they don't know what makes them special. Perhaps they are dealing with struggles at home. Maybe they are struggling at school. This may be difficult to understand, but, whatever the reason for the teasing and taunting, **it is not about you!** Sometimes people who are having a hard time are confused and think they will feel better if they just make someone else feel as bad as they do. Of course, this doesn't work—and, as a result, two people feel worse!

Second, always remember that what makes you different makes you unique and special and strong. There is only one you. No one else has your fingerprints, your exact nose, your inner-most thoughts, or . . . . You get the idea! Hold on to this thought the next time someone insults you for your differences. Better yet, thank that person for noticing. This may sound nuts, but that kid just reminded you that you are different. And being different is an awesome gift, like Dumbo's ears! The other kids will probably think you are a little crazy when you do this, but that's okay. Being a little crazy can make life fun! **You are not a mistake, and neither is anyone else.**

Pause Point *Remember back to the earlier chapters and think about what you discovered is unique about you. Is there anything about your way of being smart or creative about which you have been teased or bullied? If so, how have you handled the situation? Consider one way you're different that you were embarrassed by or didn't like that you now appreciate.*

HOW YOUR Brain WOrkS
Cingulate gyrus (sing-u-late-Ji-ris)

feeling Central or the limbic system consists of various structures that accomplish different brain tasks. These structures also tend to have really funny names. The cingulate gyrus is one.[6]

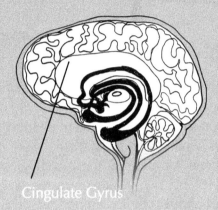

Cingulate Gyrus

The **cingulate gyrus** helps you to avoid things that will make you angry or scared. Its job is to warn you if something is about to go wrong. For the most part, the cingulate gyrus is a helpful part of your brain; it keeps you away from things that might hurt you. For example, the cingulate gyrus tells you not to touch a hot stove and not to ride your bike too fast down a big hill. Sometimes, though, the cingulate gyrus makes you scared of things you needn't be afraid of. For instance, it uses the negative memories of cultural messages about certain groups of people, called stereotypes and racism, and tells you

to be afraid of those who may fit those stereotypes. When we're open to and practice meeting new people and learning new things about others, however, our cingulate gyrus will realize that new people aren't scary. By embracing diversity, we learn not to be afraid when we encounter someone or something new.

THOUGHTS & DOODLES

Getting Through the Tough Times . . . Reimagine!

Think about the last time someone said or did something that hurt your feelings. How did it make you feel about yourself? How did it make you think about yourself? Note the incident and the thoughts and feelings you experienced.

I felt:

I felt:

I thought:

I thought:

INCIDENT!

I felt:

I felt:

I thought:

Now, look at what you wrote. Which thoughts and feelings are true and helpful? Which are not true and can be set aside? Remember that when someone is being mean, it is often more about that person's lack of social skills or their negative feelings about themselves than it is about the person they attack. Also note that sometimes feelings that might be labeled negative are working on our behalf!

THOUGHTS & FEELINGS That Are True & Helpful	THOUGHTS & FEELINGS That Are Not True & Helpful & Can Be Set Aside

Rewrite History!

Once you have finished examining the last time someone did something that hurt your feelings, rewrite history by reimagining it! With your pen or pencil, envision how you would have wanted that scene to go so that both people feel good at the end of it all? In the best-ever world, how would that incident have unfolded? Maybe even write a little movie scene that could be acted out.

Scene:

Scene:

Scene:

Scene:

Scene:

Scene:

Exploring Your Environments

We just explored accepting differences and embracing diverse cultures. **Does your experience at your school support accepting people's differences and embracing diversity,** or have your experiences at school been different from those positive messages? For example, do you see others being teased and no one doing anything about it? Maybe you're teased about your differences. If so, can you tell your teachers about the teasing and get it to stop? Write about what the environment is like at school regarding teasing.

_____

_____

_____

_____

What about at home? What messages do you hear at home about acceptance of others, no matter what they look like or what they believe? Messages of tolerance? Messages of bigotry? Do you agree with the views of your parents or siblings? Sometimes family members feel differently about tolerance. If you don't agree with your parents or siblings on tolerance issues, what might you do to change their minds—without putting yourself in danger? Write about what the environment is like at home regarding tolerance.

_____

_____

_____

Get Creative!

● **The Stereotype of Me!** Let's try a poetry activity. Think about things that people assume about you when they see you. It could be stereotypes based on your gender, your race, your religion, a physical characteristic, a personality trait, anything! You can follow the following poetry prompt to get you started. Write as many poems as you want. Then, if you feel comfortable, share your poems with friends or classmates. They may learn something new that helps them to see you and the world differently.

Just because I am   smart, it doesn't mean I am boring. I am smart AND fun!

I am not

I am not

but I am

and I am

Just because I am   ,

I am not

I am not

but I am

and I am

more thoughts

7 feeling good about yourself

Remember learning about values earlier? Do you give yourself credit for living up to your values? Do you remind yourself regularly about your unique smarts and creative gifts? Do you acknowledge and value your ability to work hard and get things done, even if it takes a long time? Do you notice and value your ability to put an outfit together and feel proud of the way you look? Do you give yourself credit for and value making things better and feel good about how you can improve things around you? Do you own your value as a friend, and are you happy when others like you? Some people can answer yes to these questions, and some people can't. Those who can't have other things they value and feel about themselves.

How you view and feel about yourself is called **self-esteem**. Remember, how you feel about yourself is directly related to how you talk to yourself in your every thought! Because we all have different thoughts about our self stored in our "interpreter," we are all giving ourselves different messages. **How one person thinks and feels about "self" may be completely different from what another person thinks and feels about "self"—because we all have unique self-talk. In** other words, we all have a personalized little voice in our head. Sometimes that voice

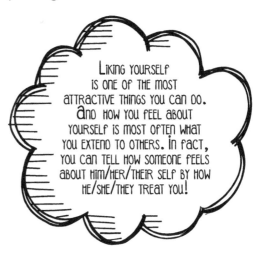

LIKING YOURSELF IS ONE OF THE MOST ATTRACTIVE THINGS YOU CAN DO. AND HOW YOU FEEL ABOUT YOURSELF IS MOST OFTEN WHAT YOU EXTEND TO OTHERS. IN FACT, YOU CAN TELL HOW SOMEONE FEELS ABOUT HIM/HER/THEIR SELF BY HOW HE/SHE/THEY TREAT YOU!

encourages and acts like the best cheerleader ever. Other times that little voice tries to take us down a notch.

Those little voices in your head let you know your values and self-esteem. They show up when you face a challenge or new situation. Maybe you decide to try playing a musical instrument. You struggle at first. You have no idea what to do. One little voice could encourage you and make you feel confident by nudging you, saying, "You just need to practice. You know you can figure this out! To learn anything new is going to take being uncomfortable, and that's okay." Or another little voice could make you feel bad with the words, "You have no idea what you are doing, and you never will!" The voices differ because there are different types of self-esteem. Two of the main types of self-esteem are the following:

> **Strong Self-Esteem:** With strong self-esteem, that voice in your head calls out the positive, helpful, and kind values. It is realistic about your strengths and weaknesses. It knows things are sometimes uncomfortable, but that doesn't make them bad. Rather, they are growth opportunities. Strong self-esteem also can help you set goals and achieve them.

> **Low Self-Esteem:** With low self-esteem, the voice in your head is negative and mean. It often focuses on your weaknesses and doesn't notice your strengths. It can make you feel like you do not matter and goes against your values. Low self-esteem also often shows up as meanness to others.

What You Think Affects Your Self-Esteem

Getting a good grade or having friends can help you feel good about yourself. But strong self-esteem comes from inside you. It comes from being proud of making choices that follow your values. This can be hard, especially if others make fun of those choices. You can feel bad about yourself and feel pressure to change, because it is natural to want to belong and have other kids like you. But that can make you do something you would not normally do. This is called **peer pressure**.

Giving in to peer pressure can make you feel good at first. Others may seem to like you more. They may act nicer toward you. You might feel more included. But if you do something against your values, part of you will feel bad about it. Because of this, you will end up having lower self-esteem. Let's look at an example of how this works: Taylor sees a classmate calling a boy mean names. She doesn't like it and thinks the behavior is mean. But then she notices her friends laughing. Because she does not want them to make fun of her, she starts laughing, too, and the boy slinks away with his head bowed. Later, Taylor feels bad about what happened. She feels mean for laughing at someone. That's because she acted against her values. She believes she should be nice to others, but she laughed anyway, because she felt peer pressure. It lowered her self-esteem!

90% OF KIDS WHO BULLY DO SO FOR ONE REASON: BECAUSE THEY BELIEVE THEIIR PEERS THINK IT'S OKAY AND BECAUSE NO ONE SAYS, "STOP!" BYSTANDERS STEPPING UP ARE THE SOLUTION TO ENDING BULLYING BEHAVIORS. FOR MORE, SEE STANDFORCOURAGE.ORG.

It takes real courage to stand up to peer pressure and be an "upstander." It can be really hard to do the right thing. In fact, our gut tends to tell us to run if someone yells at us or to be mean back when someone is mean to us. This can cause lots of trouble. In fact, your gut reaction to situations, especially stressful situations, is often wrong. For example, you might think someone is being mean when that person didn't intend to be mean.

HOW DO WE CHANGE A CULTURE OF BULLYING? WITH BYSTANDERS STEPPING UP AND SAYING "NOT COOL! WE DON'T DO THAT HERE! LET'S GO DO SOMETHING ELSE."

Because we can't always count on our thoughts (those pesky ANTs!), pausing and asking

STAND FOR COURAGE

questions can be helpful, even if we just ask those questions in our head. Having more details and learning the truth of a situation ("realistic thoughts") can stop you from saying or doing something against your values. Then you can respond based on your values instead of just reacting. "Responding" means thinking about what happened before you act rather than letting your ANTs choose how you will act. **When you respond rather than react, YOU have the power!** Plus, when you follow your own values and make choices based on them, you build strong self-esteem.

Here's something else important to remember: **Although we don't all value the same things because we are all unique, many of us do share a lot of the same values.** Think about it: Taylor probably felt pretty alone in the earlier story. She thought her classmate was being mean, but everyone else was laughing, so they must not have felt the classmate was being mean, right? Perhaps not! Maybe they just felt peer pressure to laugh, like Taylor did, and now Taylor and her friends all feel mean and alone

Pause Point *Can you think back to a time when you had strong self-esteem? What were you doing then? Maybe you were the best defender on the soccer team, absorbed in an art project, or acting as a peer counselor at school. What values, qualities, or creativity were you exercising? When you have a clear memory of your strong self-esteem in mind, try to remember what you were telling yourself then. What positive self-talk helped you feel so good about your strengths? What did your little voice inside say that made you happy? Now think of a time you didn't think so well of yourself. What was going on then? Were you getting messages from others about your values and then the little voice inside repeated those messages?*

> **Confidence** is believing in your unique self, your abilities, your judgment, and your discernment. Confidence is improved by paying attention to automatic negative thoughts and replacing them with realistic thoughts about your values, smarts, talents, and abilities. It takes confidence to fight peer pressure and do what you think is right!

for laughing. If only someone would have spoken up, it's likely a lot of the kids would not have laughed. Maybe someone even would have tried to stand up to the classmate who was being mean and prevented the other classmate from feeling really sad.

The next time you wonder if you should do something or not, pause and ask yourself a simple question: "Does it fit with my values?" If your values tell you to take a stand, listen to them! Otherwise, you'll regret your action (or lack of action) and feel poorly for ignoring your values. Saying or doing something that seems to go against the group is hard. Really hard. In the long run, though, you will feel empowered and strong if you do just that!

Standing Up to Bullying Behavior

Does all this talk about standing up to bullying behavior worry you? Do you think you will become the target or that everyone will think you're weird or annoying? It's understandable to feel uncomfortable and afraid. Don't let this stop you, though. Get creative. Think of ways to be

Sometimes you will become the target by standing up. But, like the 20th U.S. president, James Garfield, said about abolishing slavery, "I'd rather be with you defeated than against you and victorious."

true to your values without contributing to higher chances of your becoming a target. One tried-and-true method is to get a grownup when you see, hear, or experience something you feel is wrong. "Tattling" has gotten a bad rap! **Sometimes bringing an adult into the situation is the best way to help**—and it lets you stick to your values without sticking your neck out too far.

Another thing you can do is distract people or try to change the subject. Imagine Taylor's situation again, when a kid is being made fun of. What if, instead of laughing, Taylor grabbed her cool, new remote-controlled helicopter out of her backpack and started flying it around. Her classmates would

HOW YOUR BRAIN WORKS

Hypothalamus (hi – poe – THaL – a – mis)

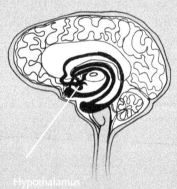

The **hypothalamus** keeps your body working. It is only the size of an almond, but it has a big voice in telling your body what to do. When your nervous system has a message for your body, that message goes through the hypothalamus, and then the hypothalamus communicates with your body by releasing hormones. Those hormones

Hypothalamus

cause your body to react in certain ways. For instance, they could send a message that says, "Your body is getting too hot! Cool down!" so you sweat or perspire. Hormones also tell your body whether or not to keep growing and even whether or not you can trust the person you are talking to. Trust creates positive feelings. We need our hypothalamus not only to trust others, but also to trust and feel positive about ourselves.[7]

probably get distracted and stop making fun of the one boy. Or, what if she yelled that she just saw a family of deer running out of the woods? This could excite the kids, so they all turn and head toward the woods. These are just a few examples. How YOU handle a situation like this will be unique to you, the things you know, and the individual way you approach the world.

The Magic of Being of Service

Just like using your "tools" of ANT trapping and standing up to bullying behavior can help you feel good about yourself, so can being of service. When we are of service to others or even animals, we learn we are needed. Knowing we are needed helps us to feel positive about ourselves and our value in the world. In other words, we feel our dignity.

Think of ways you might be of service at home. You can give your parents a break and watch your baby brother. You might set the dinner table, clear the dishes after eating, run the vacuum in the family room, or even mow the lawn. Maybe it's your job to take out the trash or feed, walk, and wash your family's dog.

Besides helping out at home, lending your time and talents to your community also can have positive impacts. At school, maybe you help the new kid get settled, start a Stand for Courage (StandForCourage.org) bullying prevention club, or organize a collection of backpacks to be sent to vulnerable migrant children through Little Mercies (LittleMercies.org). You might volunteer at your local library or help out at a local food pantry. There are lots of opportunities for youth to be of service in their own neighborhood. Ask the adults in your life for ideas and resources—and start being of service today. You'll be glad you did!

To help people have strong self-esteem, give them opportunities to be needed—even if you simply ask them to hold positive thoughts for you. We all need to be needed!

Think about it!

Being the Best You

One of the ways you can build self-esteem is to act in a way that illustrates your values. Turn back to the activity in chapter five where you listed your values. Choose three of those values and list them here. For each of the three values, explain something you have done in your life that was "in alignment" with that value. Reflecting on those actions could make you feel stronger and more confident. An extra benefit of this exercise is that you now have a list of replacement thoughts for the next time those nasty ANTs arrive to take you down a notch!

Down with Peer Pressure

➡️ When have you felt pressure to do something that was against your values? _____

➡️ In one sentence, describe the situation: _____

_____

_____

➡️ In another sentence, describe what you did:

_____

_____

_____

➡️ When this happens again, what are some of the ways you can stick to your values? Write down a bunch of ideas! Be simple and straightforward. Be silly. Be weird. Get help from others. Tell jokes. Make fun of yourself. The important thing is that you be you, the you who knows what you believe in.

_____

_____

_____

_____

_____

_____

_____

_____

_____

● **I Am!** Write an "I am" poem. Write 10 to 15 statements that start out with the phrase "I am." You may feel more proud of some of the things and less proud of others, but everything should be true. Don't forget to include ways you are different and unique, your creative talents, and your particular smarts! Here's an example to get you started.

i am wacky.
i am funny.
i am kind.
i am a student.
i am hopeful.
i am grateful for my family.
i am me.

I am _____ .

I am _____ .

I am _____ .

I am _____ .

I am _____ .

I am _____ .

I am _____ .

I am _____ .

I am _____ .

You won't always GET EVERYTHING RIGHT. BE patient. IT's THE ONLY WAY TO GROW.

8 Being mad and sad

How many times have you've yelled, "You make me so mad!" Who do you think makes you mad? Your parents? Maybe your sister or brother? Or perhaps your friend, or even your teacher! The truth is, other people can't really make you mad. Only YOU can make YOU mad!

It's now time for a review about where emotions come from. Remember:

EVENTS → INTERPRETATION → THOUGHTS → FEELINGS → ACTIONS/REACTIONS

You become mad because of how YOU view an event. This is good news, because it means YOU can manage your anger. That's not to say you won't feel the anger. You will. It's a natural emotion we all feel. In fact, sometimes it's helpful and healthy to feel angry—if what happened goes against your values and is outright wrong, like if someone says something mean.

ANGER CAN SHOW YOU WHAT'S IMPORTANT TO YOU AND SOMETIMES EVEN HELP YOU UNCOVER WHAT YOU CARE ABOUT.

What's important to know, though, is that you can stop from doing something destructive with your anger and, instead, use it to fuel a positive behavior or needed change.

self-management: working with your anger

Yep, we all get angry sometimes. In fact, feeling anger is important to humans. It's a warning signal that tells us something is wrong or just doesn't feel right. This information can be vital in protecting us. Sometimes, though, our ANTs cause us to overreact and exaggerate situations, making us angry when we don't need to be. The ANTs that really get our anger going are "Shoulds" and "Taking-Things-Too-Personally." There is even a special type of "should thought" that can really make a person angry, and that is called the "Fantasy-of-Fairness" ANT. No matter how much our parents or caregivers told us, "life isn't fair," we still think that somehow it should be. **The problem with our thinking things should work out fairly is that we really think things should work out according to what WE think is fair.** That may seem logical, but think again: It is a fantasy. Remember, there are nearly eight billion of us with our own unique version of fairness. Yikes! It's pretty clear there isn't just one standard . . . ours!

Taking things too personally can certainly trigger anger. If you interpret someone's behavior as a deliberate slight, diss, or threatening message to you, your body is wired to defend yourself. But research tells us that **about 85 percent of the time humans misinterpret and misread the intentions of others!** Literally, we are walking around feeling mad about nothing.

anger *is a big feeling, but it can be managed and it will pass. Make it pass quickly by pausing, thinking things through, and trapping those ANTs. Or use it to create change when needed! YOU get to choose your response.*

If we unleash our anger and lash out at someone, we can make a situation worse than it really is. That means that our job is to figure out whether or not we need to be angry in a particular situation and what the best way is to manage our anger. Think about being angry. What is it like? Does it feel helpful or healthy to be mad? What does that emotion trigger you to do? Do you yell? Do you stomp to your room, slam the door, and turn on really loud music? Do you throw things? Maybe you actually throw a punch! Imagine a kid is mean to you at recess. You take it too personally and then you feel mad. You are so mad that you sulk and stop having fun. The outcome? Being angry and sulking ruined your recess. Or think about a time you asked your parents for something and they said they would think about it. You told yourself it wasn't fair and then you were so mad that you yelled at them. Then they told you that you definitely were not getting what you wanted. The outcome? Your yelling stopped you from even getting anything close to what you wanted. What about when you are so mad that you say or do something mean? It might seem like you are only hurting someone else. But how do YOU feel about what you did? The outcome is usually that you feel sorry or guilty or ashamed.

In addition to sabotaging yourself, being angry can also kill your creativity. Think about the example of asking your parents or caregivers for something and they said no. What if you didn't get mad? What if you were creative about your anger and came up with some logical reasons why your parents or caregivers might see the importance of what you are asking? What if that reasoning made them say yes to what you wanted? But you'll never know, because you allowed your anger to take over your behavior.

Acting out when in the turmoil of feeling anger ends up punishing YOU—because that powerful emotion sometimes causes you to be out of control or to say and do things you regret. Doing something that hurts others makes the other person upset, and it makes YOU feel embarrassed or regretful after you have calmed down. So, how do you get anger under control?

Tips to keep you from irrationally acting out your anger

Controlling your anger is challenging work. But you can do it! Here are a few tricks that can help:

Walk away.

Walking away gives you a chance to calm down. It gives you more time to think, to get quiet and see what negative thoughts are causing your feelings. Once you redirect those thoughts to a more balanced story, you can make a better choice.

Ask for space.

If you're angry and can't walk away, ask the other person to give you space. You might say: "I need time to calm down. Can you, please, leave me alone right now?" or "Can we talk about this later? I need some space right now." It can be helpful to reassure the person you'll be right back and that you care about the relationship, if this is true.

Take 5 . . . deep breaths.

Invite yourself to take five deep breaths. Then respond. This gives you time to think, and it also can help calm down your body. Breathe in through your nose and out through your mouth.

Draw or write about your anger.

Get your feelings out on paper. Write about what you're feeling, or create a drawing that shows how you feel. You might come up with something surprisingly artistic. Then, try ripping up and throwing away the story or drawing. This can help you let go of angry feelings, so you don't act on them.

Do something to calm yourself.

When you're so angry you can't think straight, set aside the thoughts upsetting you and turn to trying to soothe yourself. What works? Does walking help you to settle your anger? Does curling up with a special stuffed animal help? Does jumping rope calm your nerves? What about playing an instrument or listening to music? Do whatever makes you settle back into your true self. When you feel better, you'll be able to approach the situation that made you angry in a way in which you'll feel more proud.

Show yourself compassion.

Tell yourself, "This is really hard. I can do better and so can they. I can get through this!"

Remember your values.

If you do something that hurts others and it makes you feel bad, you are acting against your values. You are not being the person you want to be. Before you react, pause, think about your values, and list them in your head.

Get silly.

Sometimes you might feel so mad you want to throw a punch. That means your emotion is so strong it wants to come out physically. To deal with this powerful desire, some people find it helpful to hit a pillow. You might also try something even more fun: Get silly! Make a funny face. Shake your anger off like a wet dog shakes off water! Do jumping jacks. Dance a goofy dance. Sing "Happy Birthday." Being wacky can change what your brain focuses on. Be creative. Find your own kind of wacky that helps you express and overcome that angry feeling. Maybe you can even come up with your "go-to move" for every time you get angry. That silly move might help you stop listening to the ANTs of anger in an instant!

Ask for change.

If you're angry about a friend being racist, it's appropriate to be angry and then to help create change. You can do this by being honest about how the racism makes you feel and then by requesting the change you want to see. Maybe your friend doesn't want to change; you can't control anyone but yourself. At this point, you can decide if having a friend with values different than your own works or if you can grow together and teach one another.

Humor *is our ability to laugh and make others laugh. Believe it or not, it is one of the most powerful resources we have as humans. It can transform almost any situation!*

How Your Brain Works
amygdala (a – mig – da – la)

The **amygdala** is the part of the brain's limbic system that can make you feel fear.[8] We've had this part of our brain since our ancestors were cave dwellers, and it was very important to them. When cave dwellers were at risk of losing their food or shelter, the amygdala's job was to take over their brain and put them on

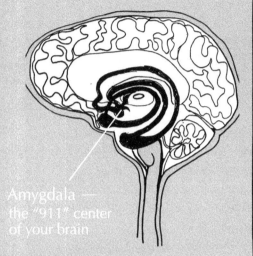

Amygdala — the "911" center of your brain

automatic pilot so they would quickly get afraid and fight for things such as the food, water, and shelter they needed to survive.

Today, however, most of us have the things we need to survive. Our amygdala, however, still wants to take over when we're afraid. If you're faced with something that scares you, the amygdala may send messages to the rest of your body to fight, flee, freeze, or appease. Those messages can cause you to get red in the face or your heart will start beating really fast. You might even have the urge to scream. All these reactions are caused by your brain responding to the fear. If, instead, you can quickly tell your amygdala, "No! I'm not afraid," then you can stop feeling afraid—and avoid all the negative physical and emotional reactions.

No! I'm not afraid!

I'm in control.

Think for a minute.

I've got this!

Dealing with Depression

Like getting angry, feeling sad is a normal part of life. You may feel sad if you lose a basketball game, a friend disappointed you, or you break a favorite something. When you feel sad, it's important to remember that sadness is completely worthy of respect. It is also temporary, although it might last what seems like a long time.

Sometimes, though, when you feel sad, you also may tell yourself stories that make the sadness worse. When you tell yourself it is hopeless, that you are helpless to change how you feel, that today's challenge is part of a pattern of endless challenges, and that you are a bad person, your sadness may have turned to depression. Signs that you are depressed include:

➡ **You stop playing or doing other things that used to be fun.**

➡ **You do not want to be around people.**

➡ **You feel tired a lot.**

➡ **You are slower when talking or moving, or you cannot sit still.**

➡ **It is hard to remember, concentrate, or decide anything.**

➡ **You sleep too much or too little.**

➡ **You are not interested in food and may lose weight, or you might overeat.**

➡ **You have pain, but no one knows what is causing it and it does not go away.**

Depression is serious. If you are worried about it, talk to an adult you trust. This can be one of your parents, a teacher, coach, school counselor, or relative.

What kinds of things can trigger thoughts that make you depressed? It's different for everyone. Part of being a unique human being is that your thoughts and emotions are unique to you, and this

> **Did you know** that lots of creative people suffer from depression? Artists. Musicians. Writers. Actors. Many of them use their creativity to work through, learn to live with, or put their depression to work for them. So doodle or paint. Start writing a story, poem, or song. Come up with some dance moves that reflect how you're feeling. Letting your creative side go wild can be a great way to ease depression's sad feelings.

reality can cause you to feel lonely at times. What matters is how you interpret an event, how those thoughts cause you to feel, how YOUR life is impacted by your feelings.

If you think you're depressed, among the most important values to remember is acceptance. **Acceptance means admitting that something is wrong. It also means being willing to accept help**—because anyone suffering from depression needs to be able to reach out to others for effective support. Challenges of mental health are not something of which to feel ashamed!

One of the most important tools to remember if you think you're depressed is ANT control. Although when you are depressed it is best to get the help of a professional such as your school counselor, you can help yourself right away by grabbing a sheet of paper and creating an "ANT elimination journal." First write down all your negative thoughts, no matter how big or small. Leave space below each thought. Now look at the ANTs listed in chapter four. Under each thought take a guess at which ANT is involved. It might be more than one. Once you have done this step, you can clearly see the new story emerge of what you need to say to yourself to replace a particular ANT. The next step is to write down those replacement thoughts and see if you feel better. After all that writing, there is one more step: Ask yourself, "Is there a particular action I can take about the things bothering me?" Then do it!

in need of Deep Healing?

When you are cared for with unconditional love and your caregivers meet your physical, social, and emotional needs, you feel safe, secure, and connected. According to research, that sense of belonging can support you to take on life's challenges, enhancing your get-through-it grit when you encounter hardship. In fact, one of the best predictors of optimal well-being, along with future success, is sensing that you belong, that you are included, needed, and connected to others around you.

Unfortunately, many people have their lives derailed by traumatic events such as migration, poverty, community or domestic violence, discrimination, disability, war, or other painful life circumstance. These events can be happening in the present or could have happened in the past; it doesn't matter. They can impact individuals, families, even whole communities, creating a collective and sometimes historical trauma.

Traumatic events and historical trauma are truly frightening and overwhelming. Children and families who live with trauma may live in a state of constant fear. They also may lack basic needs such as food, shelter, and health care. Their fears and concerns are very real and sometimes extremely dire. Although communities might have supportive resources, people do not always have access to those resources or the knowledge of how to access the resources, so traumatized people will need strong support and deep healing.

If you are experiencing trauma, reach out and talk to a teacher,  school counselor, or trusted friend who can help you find the support you need. This book looks at how to develop your potential to be the best you possible, and sometimes that means seeking in-person help. If you are not experiencing trauma, learn more about the topic and find ways you can help others feel safe and connected. In service, we all build a sense of belonging.

HOW YOUR BRAIN WORKS
HIPPOCAMPUS (HIP- O - CAM - PIS)

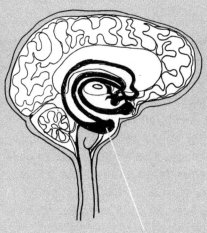

Hippocampus

The hippocampus is a part of the limbic system. It's in charge of holding memories. In fact, it especially likes to hold memories from long ago, when you were very little. Scientists have learned that the hippocampus also makes us feel sad sometimes. People who are depressed have a smaller hippocampus than people who do not have depression.[9]

If you are depressed, that doesn't mean there is something wrong with you. Everyone's brain is unique, so everyone has different emotions. If you have a brain that tends toward depression, however, you may need to stay on your toes and really pay attention to your self-talk. Learning ANT categories and how to replace those negative thoughts will be super important.

On a lighter note, here is a funny fact about the hippocampus: It looks like a seahorse, and *Hippocampus* is actually the Latin word for seahorse.

Think about it!

Game Plan

Think about something that makes you mad. Remember, getting mad is not a problem. Everyone gets mad from time to time, and sometimes being angry motivates us to do good in the world. Sometimes, though, the way we get mad or what we do when we get mad tends to go against our values. Having a game plan about how we can calm down before we do something we regret is a way we can hold onto our values, even when we get mad.

Use this space to write down what you might do to keep from losing control and doing something destructive the next time something happens that will make you mad. This can involve thinking of at least three values you want to have in your "back pocket" the next time you get mad.

_____

_____

_____

_____

_____

_____

_____

_____

Getting a Handle on Sadness

Label the following statements as true (T) or false (F):

T or **F** Sadness comes and goes.

T or **F** It is unhealthy to feel sad.

T or **F** Depression will go away by itself.

T or **F** If you feel depressed, you should talk to an adult.

Answer Key: T, F, F, T

Now, write about a problem or situation that tends to make you sad.
Write down all the things you cannot do to solve it. Then go back and think of all the things you can do to solve it, even if they are small. How does it feel to have some ways to make a difference in your sadness figured out ahead of time? Remember that it's okay to feel sad!

_____

_____

_____

_____

_____

_____

_____

_____

_____

_____

_____

GET Creative!

● **Let It Flow!** If you are able, get a newspaper and open it up so you have a large surface of paper to work on in case your art for this activity overflows the page. If you don't have a newspaper, work on a surface that can be cleaned easily and use only non-permanent markers or paints. (Or use colored pencils or crayons on the open space below on this page.) In the center of the opened newspaper, put a piece of art paper. Choose markers or paint colors that make you feel relaxed. Only use those colors. Put on calming music; you might even want to try classical music as an experiment. Get a marker or paint brush in your hand and place your other hand on the piece of art paper (or on this book) so you know where it is. Close your eyes and just let your creativity flow to the rhythm of the music. Then open your eyes and discover what you created! Try adding another color if you'd like or start again with a new piece of paper.

creative space!

9 anxiety, worry, & panic, oh, my!

Believe it or not, the feeling of anxiety is meant to protect humans. Early cave people needed to stay vigilant about intruders and predators. Today, although most of us live relatively non-threatened lives, we still need to be prepared for all kinds of things—for school quizzes, for not falling off our bikes, for not letting the neighborhood squirrel bite us. So, a little anxiety can be helpful, keeping us vigilant to stay safe and do well in school and in life in general. **But sometimes—through the way we think—we create, reinforce, and exaggerate our stress-related problems to the point of harming ourselves and others.**

Imagine this: You get to school in the morning. Your friend asks if you're ready for the math test. Your eyes go wide. Your heart beats faster. You have trouble breathing. You forgot to study! The test does not go well—and you really wanted to do well in math. Now you get a sick feeling every time you arrive at school. What if you forget another test? This feeling is called "anxiety." Although a little anxiety about tests is normal and based on a real and justifiable concern, if you study regularly and do your homework, there is no reason for anything negative to occur. That means you need not always be afraid something bad will happen, which can help to keep you from feeling anxious all the time.

Anxiety is the close cousin of depression. In fact, depression and anxiety are two sides of the same coin. The coin these two share is over-estimating the risks of a situation or event (Remember our ANT companions Blowing-Things-Up, Jumping-to-Conclusions, and All-or-Nothing Thinking?) and under-estimating your ability to cope with the situation.

Anxious ANTs tells you the worst will likely happen, and depression ANTs tell you it's hopeless and even worse: that it's YOUR fault!

Anxiety starts with thinking worried thoughts. You worry about failing tests. You worry about being picked last in gym class games. You worry about kids making fun of you. You may have these worries because something negative happened once and you're scared it will happen again. Or maybe you watched a TV show or read a book in which something bad happened, and now you're worried it will happen to you.

Interestingly, your anxiety may have originated in a real situation, but then it extended to areas where it isn't justified, into areas where you feel you have no control or power to change things or be prepared. Your ANTs are telling you a story that the future holds DANGER, and you will be powerless to do anything! But you now have powerful tools that will help you to cope with many of the challenges life brings your way. Your newest superpower is using ANT traps!

Really bad moments of anxiety are called panic attacks or anxiety attacks. You become so worried you can feel it in your body. Your breathing might speed up. Your heart may race. You might start shaking or sweating. You may feel pain in your chest. Your vision may change, with everything feeling closed in, like a tunnel. You even might feel like you are going to throw up. Your anxiety may become so persistent that it's disabling—and less pin-pointed to a specific worry-inducing event. Are you curious about how and why this happens? See "How the Brain Works" on page 108 that explains how the hypothalamus in the brain serves as the connection between emotions like anxiety and the physical body.

YOU can't 100 percent know how something is ever going to turn out until it actually happens. It's kind of like how the weather person can't always precisely predict the weather. That's why you need to keep anxiety under control, because if you don't, you can end up in full-blown panic mode.

What you can Do to reduce anxiety

Dealing with anxiety requires two things: **preparation paired with balanced thinking**. The way this magic mixture works is that, when you start thinking about how poorly everything is going, you'll catch yourself and use your new tool to remind yourself which ANTs are in control, give yourself some positive and balanced thoughts to replace those ANTs, and check in to see what you need to do to be prepared for the situation. Then, feeling a bit more positive prevents you from falling into the trap of worry and panic.

A great place to start with preventing anxiety, worry, and panic is to know what particular situations make you anxious. Once you can identify those, you can prepare for them: Study for the test. Finish your homework. Practice your swing. Play that piano piece over and over.

Plan ahead for the week. Know where you're going and how you're going to get there. Ask questions. Lots of them!

Here's another powerful tool for preparing for challenging situations: Using your imagination to think positive thoughts. If an upcoming situation has you crawling with worry ANTs, try this exercise. First, close your eyes and take five deep, slow breaths and open your imagination. Imagine that things go well. Imagine that you do well. Imagine how you will handle problems that might arise. Be aware, though, that what works to calm you and make you feel in control might not be what works for someone else, because everyone is unique. So play around and try different things. Make up a story about what will happen and write it down. Draw pictures of different outcomes. Make up a poem or a song about the situation. Or create a list of ways you can prepare and reasons why you won't be anxious.

What works for you might seem silly, but who cares? **The point is that your thought-through coping strategy just might work.** Most times, being a little silly can be a big help, too. It can make you realize the situation isn't as serious as it feels when you're anxious or panicking. Basically, preparing helps you to change the way you react when anxiety tries to take over. It allows you to focus on the positive fact that you are prepared.

In sum, it's the negative thoughts that cause anxiety, so the key is to push away and replace those negative thoughts with positive, realistic thoughts. That said, though, there are many things we can't control. **Sometimes the best we can do is learn to live with those things while still striving for a high quality life.** Remember,

much about which we worry never happens. If it does, we use our unique smarts and creative problem-solving skills to manage the situation. We rock our ability to own our thoughts, actions, and behavior. After much practice, many trials and errors, this mindful approach to living can become your default mode and possibly save you from much unnecessary turmoil.

At the first sign of feeling anxious try this process:

➡️ Listen and pay attention to your thoughts. Thank them for trying to help you and say, "I've got this from here!" Then write down all those thoughts you identify as negative.

➡️ Use the ANT categories in this book to help you identify the thoughts causing your fear. In other words, find out what you fear.

➡️ Now think of a balanced, realistic thought that "talks back" to each of the ANTs. Write that down too.

➡️ Ask yourself, "Is there any action I need to take in order to feel less worried?"

➡️ Tell yourself, "This is hard, but I'll get through it."

For example, imagine your teacher says you will have a test tomorrow. You worry you will fail the test. Your first step can be to pay extra attention and listen to your thoughts. The first ones tell you that you failed the last test (a fact) and that you are not smart (Uh, oh! "Labeling" ANT!). Instead of going into a full panic attack, you can pause and decide to fight that ANT with a balanced view of the facts: The truth is that you did not study for the last test you failed, but 1) you do not fail every test, and 2) you prepared, asked for help, and studied this time! Because you prepared and the facts all point to a positive outcome, you can replace your ANT with the positive facts of: "I can get a decent grade. I don't have to panic. I see that the action I need to take to help me feel better is to study more tonight and ask my mom to quiz me." Eventually, this approach will start to calm you.

Take Deep, Slow Belly Breaths

Another way to calm yourself is with deep, slow belly breaths. Put your hands on your belly. Close your eyes. Breathe in and let your belly rise. Then breathe out and feel it empty out. Breathe in through your nose and out through your mouth. (Do this slowly and calmly, because big breaths might lead to hyperventilation and lightheadedness, which you don't want!) Count backwards from twenty

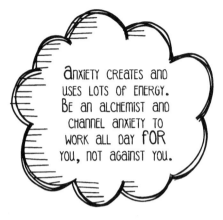

anxiety creates and uses lots of energy. Be an alchemist and channel anxiety to work all day for you, not against you.

to zero while you keep doing this. Belly breathing does many things such as 1) it can distract your mind from your anxiety, and 2) it can help get rid of negative feelings in your body such as pain in your chest or dizziness.

Or Try a Wacky Approach!

Want a fun way to kick anxiety to the curb? Play a game called "What's the Worst That Can Happen?" Here's how you play: The next time you start to feel anxious about something, think about the worst possible outcome. Go overboard. Exaggerate. Eventually your ideas will start to seem so silly that the situation won't seem so scary. For instance, consider how scared you are of failing that test. The feeling makes you want to run away. But how horrible could it actually be? Imagine the worst: The test could be in a different language. You could get every question wrong, even your name. The whole class could find out you failed. And it doesn't stop there. Maybe the kids on the bus build a

rocket to shoot you into space so you have to live with Martians! Pretty silly, right? Are you still feeling anxious? Or are you caught up in this ridiculous story of getting kicked off the planet for failing a test? Probably the second choice. Laughing a little at yourself and your fears makes it a whole lot easier to see that your ANTs are making you scared. Your "real" fears are just as made up as your story. Shake them off! Literally, move your body and shake off your worries and fears.

anxiety's many Disguises

Sometimes anxiety shows up as something else—
things like:

- anger

- difficulty sleeping

- defiance

- flying off the handle

- lack of focus

- avoidance

- negativity

- overplanning

Recognize and call out anxiety for what it is!
If you can label it, some of its power is zapped!

How Your Brain Works

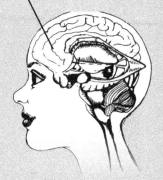

The **prefrontal cortex** is that part of your brain that helps to observe a situation or person and make decisions based on those observations. It does this by considering what you see, scanning your memories for similar or related information, and then trying to figure out what is the best thing to do next—all faster than a blink! In other words, your brain makes decisions based on what is happening and what you remember happening in the past. When the "interpreter" part of your brain remains neutral and doesn't tell you to guard yourself, then you can make decisions from a place of compassion, peace, and safety.

Another important job of the prefrontal cortex is **impulse control**. That is your ability to choose how you will respond, rather than just reacting—like a time when you ate too many cookies because you couldn't stop yourself, when you jumped into a group teasing someone because it seemed like a good idea, or when you shoved your brother when you knew you would get in trouble. It's much better to respond from a values-based place than just to react without pausing and thinking!

It's good to know about the important jobs of the prefrontal cortex because sometimes it needs help. When the "interpreter" tells you stories that make you anxious, worried, angry, scared, or something negative like that, your amygdala (the "911" emergency room) overreacts and takes over, putting you into flight, fight, freeze, or appease mode. Some brain scientists, called neuroscientists, call this "flipping your lid." When you flip your lid, you can't access your prefrontal cortex, which means you won't be able to make good decisions, put the brakes on unhealthy or risky behavior, or have any kind of emotional balance. By using belly breaths, checking your thoughts for ANTs, and replacing the ANTs with balanced and positive thoughts, you can calm the amygdala and get your wise, wonderful prefrontal cortex working again.[10]

Think about it!

Recognizing Anxiety

Circle the potential symptoms of anxiety.

Breathing too fast	swollen tongue	sweating
Racing heart	shaking	upset stomach
itching	bruising	hair falling out
pain in your chest		dizziness

Answer Key for Anxiety Symptoms: Breathing too fast, racing heart, pain in your chest, shaking, sweating, upset stomach

Making Anxiety Work for You

Know that the other side of any negative is a positive, and that there's a gift to be summoned if you learn how!

To tackle anxiety and make it work for you, write down several situations that make you anxious. For example, maybe you get anxious before a piano recital, when talking with someone in particular, or before a big game. Next to each situation, write a plan of action. What trick will you use to try to overcome your anxious feelings? How will you make anxiety work for you?

SITUATION

Plan of Action! Reimagine!

_____
_____
_____
_____
_____

Plan of Action! Reimagine!

_____
_____
_____
_____
_____

SITUATION

SITUATION

Plan of Action! Reimagine!

_____
_____
_____
_____
_____

Plan of Action! Reimagine!

_____
_____
_____
_____

SITUATION

GET Creative

● Shake My Stresses Away! Much like with anxiety, some stress is just extra energy. Make it work for you! Think of a song you really like and know really well. Then change the words to make it a song to use when you feel anxious. What messages will help you to shake off the anxiety and realize your strength and resilience? What do you wish someone would say to you to calm you and let you know you are loved and safe and capable? Write those messages into your song. It could be silly or serious or dramatic. Doesn't matter! What matters is, it's YOUR song to sing to yourself any time you need it. You'll be expending your extra energy and leaving behind the stress.

10 Your Shield: is it Real? is it Kind?

Something else to know that can help you to be your best self is that all people put "shields" in front of themselves. On the front of each of our shields is a particular image of who we want others to think we are. That image, or "projection," is made up of actions and words.

Think about your shield like this: If someone put sticky notes on a picture of you to describe you, what would those sticky notes say? Sassy, athletic, happy, musical, loud, a dancer, a good reader, smart, quiet, kind, friendly, mean, sad, helpful, a nerd, joyful, mom's little helper? Remember, the sticky notes say how others see you, not who you might really be. The big question is, how did others get those ideas about you? They either saw you do things (actions) or heard you say things (words) to make them think this way about you.

> Sometimes we design and put up our shield knowingly or "consciously." Sometimes we do this without realizing we are doing it, which is called doing it "unconsciously."

Your shield projection, the way others see you, can be either positive or negative and have positive or negative consequences. On the good side, if your shield tells others, for example, that you are brave, loving, and kind, others might want to hang out with you. But, if you choose words and actions that create a shield that says you are afraid of others, that you don't like to try new things, that you are mean, or that life is no fun, then making friends might be hard for you and you might become really lonely. Think about it this way: **Your actions and words, things YOU control, are the keys to how other people see you**. But you can't ever really control what others think about you or how they treat you! All you can do is **attempt** to control how they think and feel about you through your shield projection. Beware, though, if you try to control others' thoughts of you, you might end up sacrificing your authentic self you wish you could show others.

using your Shield for protection . . . or to Hide

Just like our shield projections are sometimes positive and sometimes negative, some of the ways we use our shields are healthy, and some of them are not. A shield that tells others we can be strong can be really valuable in protecting us; it can help us get through a difficult day or a stressful situation. For example, maybe your grandmother is sick and, although you're sad about it, you don't want to talk about it. So, putting up a shield that says, "I'm okay today," can keep others from asking questions until you're ready to talk.

Similarly, sometimes we unknowingly, or unconsciously, use our shield to hide what we see as our weaknesses. This might distract others from our insecurities and maybe help us feel safe from the judgment of others. Consider a situation when Damon thought he needed to have his friends see him as a "tough guy," so he pretended he liked to bike ride really fast. He even told other kids that his nickname was Rough Rider and that he had won some races. Although they weren't true, those things were a part of Damon's shield. Sadly, Damon wasn't a really great bike rider because he hadn't had the chance to ride too often. Reality hit as he slammed the pavement in front of all his buddies—who would have liked him even if he wasn't a great bike rider—but they didn't want to trust him after he lied to them about his biking ability.

The bottom line is, if we use our shields to keep parts of who we are hidden, this might prevent us from building a deep, true connection with others. A positive "redo" on Damon's part might be to say to his friends, "I really want to be a great cyclist. I'm still working on it."

Removing Your Shield with Trust

Everyone has a shield. When you meet someone for the first time, most of what you see of that person's identity is really that person's shield, and that's okay. You do the same thing when introducing yourself to others; you often offer your shield as the real you, yet it is only a part of the real you, the part you're willing to show. It is usually only when you are fortunate enough to develop trust that you will feel safe enough to remove your shield entirely (you can always put it back on) and let someone know the "full" you. It's in our vulnerability that we find the healthiest connection with others.

So, how do you develop trust? It comes after:
- → **spending lots of time learning about each other,**
- → **learning we are safe in each other's company,**
- → **being confident you each can count on the other, and**
- → **most importantly, trusting yourself and your own value whether others see it or not.**

Some people are **"heart-led,"** with kindness, respect, and compassion (for self and others) being their most important values, the values that drive their behavior. Because you feel their goodness right away, trusting heart-led people can happen quickly. What's really cool is that YOU can decide to be heart-led and become an easy-to-trust person! Ultimately, though, developing trust is a process. And it always begins with being open to sharing and caring and with trusting in yourself.

Trust your own value, and others will learn to trust you too.

Your Online Shield

If you play video games or use online social media platforms to communicate with others, you also have another possible way of putting up a shield in front of yourself. In games, this might be called your "avatar." As you know, your **avatar** is the electronic image representing you in virtual space. Sometimes you get to design your own avatar, picking only characteristics you'd like others to see. When you do this, the people with whom you play the games get to see what you want them to see. Unlike with real people, they never get to see the real you.

The same goes for texting and social-networking on electronic devices. You get to control what you say and what pictures you post. But, honestly, don't you try to only say really good things about yourself or post only the very best pictures of yourself? Don't you try to make yourself look perfect? That's called "air-brushing." It's like having an absolutely perfect shield that is always shiny and bright. Almost everybody does this on computers! But the truth is: People are never perfect. We all have some things that are attractive about ourselves and some things we might like to improve. We don't always look great in photos. Everybody has an off hair day once in a while. We are all human!

That means that, when we are communicating with someone online, we are never interacting with who a person really is. We are just seeing that person's shield, and that shield might be all made-up stuff! That's why it's so important to be careful of trusting people you meet online.

Another thing to think about is that it can be super easy to forget who you really are if you are spending a lot of time on screens using a made-up avatar or fake shield. **Being the best YOU takes lots of practice with real people, lots of making mistakes and learning from them in real time, and a ton of bravery to show your true colors in all their glory . . . in all their mess . . . in all their evolution.**

(Pause Point) *Who are the people you trust most in the world who know the most about your "full" self? How did you learn you were safe in their company? Think about the ones you haven't known from birth. What risks have you taken to show them your most real self? When did you try to reveal a part of your true self and it didn't go so well?*

THOUGHTS & DOODLES

Think about it!

Exploring Your Shield

What might your shield be hiding? Do some parts of your shield not represent the real you? Describe the differences between the two: your shield that you show people and the real you.

My Shield	Less Known Parts of the Real Me

Using Your Shield for Protection

What is one time when your shield protected you?
Explain how it did that.

_____

_____

_____

_____

_____

_____

_____

_____

_____

_____

_____

_____

_____

_____

_____

Your Circle of Trust

Make a list of people you trust and who you let see all of you,
the real you.

_____   _____

_____   _____

_____   _____

_____   _____

_____   _____

GET Creative!

My Shield and Me! Draw two shields, or better yet, make two shields. If you want to make them, you can use cardboard from a cereal box, markers, glitter, glue, paint, and the like. One of the shields will show what you let others see of you; the other shield will show what that first shield is hiding of you. Think about (and maybe write about) why you might be hiding some parts of yourself and what it might feel like if you let others see those hidden parts.

creative space!

more creative space!

REMEMBER, HOW OTHERS THINK ABOUT YOU IS MORE ABOUT WHO THEY ARE THAN WHO YOU ARE!

11 The Power of Compassion

Compassion is a way of being with others in which you show you care about them, want to understand their reality, and feel kindly toward them. It is your concern when you see others suffer. It motivates you to want to help. Being compassionate has many benefits. Compassion can stop you from hurting other people. It can help you to make life better for everyone. And being compassionate also can make YOU feel happier. **People who are more compassionate feel more peaceful, relaxed, and happy than those who are not as compassionate.**

In a way, when you are kind to others, you are also being kind to yourself. That's because, if you are compassionate toward others, being compassionate toward yourself comes more easily. With self-compassion, when you make a mistake, you will be better at forgiving yourself. When you struggle with something, you will be more patient and kinder to yourself. This is important, because we all struggle from time to time. Sometimes it may seem like you are struggling more than others, but it could be that you are jumping to conclusions. Remember that ANT? The truth is that all kids mature at their own pace, so some classmates might be developing faster than you in one area or another. It's perfectly okay! You just have to keep trying and not be afraid to ask for help. Practicing self-compassion can make this situation easier. You can forgive yourself for the bumps in your road. And you can focus on using your creativity to find new and exciting paths just for you!

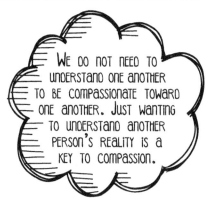

We do not need to understand one another to be compassionate toward one another. Just wanting to understand another person's reality is a key to compassion.

a very wise man, *Marshall Rosenberg, once said: ". . . [T]he more I empathize with [others] and their needs, the more likely I am to get my own needs met." What he is saying is that an important way to be the happiest, best YOU possible is by seeing the world from someone else's perspective and having compassion, even for yourself.*

HOW DO YOU BECOME MORE COMPASSIONATE?

Being compassionate can be challenging. You can get caught up in your own problems, negative thinking, and destructive feelings. But developing self-compassion and compassion for others is worth it! It will make you and the world stronger and happier. Compassion can help you remember that we all have a place in the world, and that each of our lives is just our own personal classroom for learning to be our best self. Instead of shutting people out, you can invite them in. **The more you listen to other people's perspectives without judging them, the more you build your own deeper understanding.** Ultimately, the healthier and happier you will be!

Here are a few things you can do to become more compassionate:

1. Pretend you are in someone else's shoes.

Imagine what it's like to be another person. If a girl at school always sits by herself at lunch and doesn't seem to have any friends, avoiding her can be too easy. Maybe she is a "loner" because her parents do not speak English at home and she is just learning the language herself. Think about what it would be like to be her, sitting in classes and then listening to all the other kids in the cafeteria talking so fast. She may only be picking up words here and there. This new understanding may help you be brave enough to invite her to join you and your friends at your table—and to ask her about herself, talking very slowly. She might become a friend and introduce you to all kinds of fascinating things about her culture, all because you decided to consider what life might be like for her.

2. Notice if you are judging people and situations.

Another way to use the tool of ANT control is for creating acceptance and tolerance. This means you notice Labeling and Should ANTs. They are the opposite of compassion. If you are thinking about others with a negative filter, challenge yourself to replace those thoughts with neutral ones. "She looks icky in those pants" is not compassionate, but "She has a right to wear what makes her feel good about herself, just as I do" is a thought that moves you into acceptance.

3. Practice forgiveness.

Compassion is at the root of practicing forgiveness. Some people think forgiving others makes you weak, but this is not so. It's easy to hold on to anger; it's forgiving that takes courage and strength. It also can take a long time. Some people work for years and years to forgive another! You must be strong to move forward. You must be brave to trust someone again. The more you practice forgiveness, the more compassionate a person you will become.

4. Read a good book or watch a good movie.

Fiction is a powerful tool for expanding our ability to be compassionate. A good book or movie transports you into the minds and experiences of other people. You imagine their inner world as  you try to understand their behavior and what motivates each character to do the things they do and how they do them. This can help you build your own skills in the real world and know yourself even better.

5. Learn something from everyone.

You do not have to be friends with everyone. You do not have to like everyone. But you can learn something from everyone. Compassion can help. Here's an example: Connor pushed Moses hard in line. Moses was angry and thought Connor was being very mean. But then Moses caught himself and remembered the importance of being compassionate. Instead of pushing Connor back, he took a few deep breaths and asked Connor to explain why he pushed him. It turns out that Moses had stepped on Connor's foot without Moses even realizing it! So Moses apologized and Connor also apologized—for overreacting. Now both boys felt better. Also, Moses learned to watch where he was stepping, and Connor learned that pushing is not the right way to respond. Because Moses braved practicing compassion, both boys learned something.

HOPE is a belief that good things can happen. Hope is the replacement thought for many ANTs. So powerful at fighting ANT infestations, hope is like an enormous ANT trap! Thoughts of hope are ones that talk back to your negative spin and that of others, especially when it comes to the ANTs of Blowing-Things-Up, Ignoring-the-Good, and Jumping-to-Conclusions. When you are compassionate, you can give others hope, and that creates a better world.

6. Reach out to others.

Part of being compassionate is wanting to help. You can defend classmates being picked on. You can assist a struggling classmate. You can cheer up someone who is feeling down. Yes! Kids can do all these things and more! If you are unsure about how you might help someone else, ask an adult because adults have a lot of experience and can be a good source of advice. But sometimes it just takes a kid to fix a problem! You have a unique perspective as a kid. You have a perspective that adults don't have anymore. You may be able to see a problem before an adult does. You may have a unique way to help that an adult would not think of. That doesn't mean you must go it alone. And you should not intervene if you are afraid for your safety. But it does mean that you should trust yourself and your judgment. If you are coming from a place of compassion, then you are likely doing the right thing.

7. Practice self-compassion.

Self-compassion is key! One trick in tough situations is to say quietly to yourself, "I know this is hard and hurts, but I'll be okay."

Pause Point   Who do you know who shows a lot of compassion? What is it you see in those people? How do they go about showing kindness and understanding toward others? When was a time you needed compassion and received it? When have you made an attempt at showing compassion, directly or indirectly? How did it go? What were you left thinking and feeling?

How Your Brain Works

The **ventral tegmentum** is an area of the limbic system of your brain that remembers the things you like.[11] For example, maybe you like strawberry ice cream. This is because your ventral tegmental area remembers you had positive feelings the last time you ate strawberry ice cream. Now when you see or smell strawberry ice cream, your brain quickly tells you that you want to eat the strawberry ice cream so you have those positive feelings again.

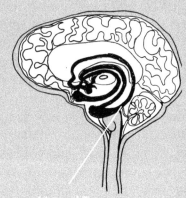

Ventral Tegmentum

Well, a similar thing happens when you say and do kind things for other people. Your ventral tegmentum will remember how good it feels to do and say kind things for other people. It will then tell you to keep doing helpful things for other people, so you will feel good inside afterward.

By doing and saying kind things, you teach your ventral tegmental area that you like doing those things, so you end up doing them more and more. That's a really positive thing for those who are receiving your goodness as well as for YOU—because you end up being happier.

another *totally cool thing about the brain is that it doesn't know the difference between giving a compliment and receiving a compliment. If you say something thoughtful to someone else, YOUR brain floods with the chemicals of feeling good just like it does when someone says something kind to you.*

THOUGHTS & DOODLES

Think about it!

We All Make Mistakes! All of Us!

Think of a mistake you recently made that still bothers you. Describe in a few sentences what happened. Next, write down the words you said to yourself when you made the mistake. If you would prefer to draw a comic strip of the event and use speech bubbles for the dialogue, go for it!

MISTAKE
_____
_____
_____

What Happened: _____
_____
_____
_____
_____
_____

What I Said To Myself: _____
_____
_____
_____
_____

The Outcome: _____
_____
_____
_____
_____

Things to consider are: Were you kind to yourself? Were you compassionate? Were you understanding? If so, great. If not, write a new script! Either draw a new comic strip or write a new paragraph that shows how you will talk to yourself the next time you make a mistake. How can you use words to be kind to yourself, encourage yourself, and show you understand that everyone makes mistakes—that mistakes are the way we learn to become better human beings.

A Different Perspective!

Write a story from another perspective. Choose a movie, book, TV show episode, or real life story you know well. Think of whose perspective you will use to tell the story. Fill in the blanks below to get started.

Movie/book/real life story/TV show episode:

_____

_____

Whose perspective or point of view is the story told from as you know it?

_____

_____

Choose a character who is in the story but is not a main character and tell the story from this particular character's point of view. _____

_____

_____

_____

For example, maybe you're writing a newspaper story about schools named after someone who owned slaves. How might someone whose ancestors were slaves view the renaming of those schools? What might be that person's perspective about the controversy? Or, how might Robin tell a Batman story from his own perspective? Better yet, maybe you had a fight with someone in your family and you'll write about that fight. Whatever situation or subject you choose, use the next page or a notebook to tell the story, but from a different person's or character's point of view.

12 you can do it!

We've explored a lot in this book how to figure out who you are and what your gifts to the world might be. A big question of this ongoing journey is, how do you know when you're on the right path to your best self? Getting to a sense of being on the path to your best self will have its twists and turns, perhaps many bumps along the way. In fact, we all stray off the path now and again.

One of the ways to make progress toward being your best self is by trying to reach a state of paying attention to any and all ANTs. It's called **living with intention.** This involves being aware of or paying attention to things such as how you're feeling physically and emotionally when you do something. Ultimately, "living with intention" means making choices in a way that your future self will appreciate.

For example, if you have peanut allergies, would it be wise to eat a peanut butter and jelly sandwich? No way! So you intentionally are careful about not eating anything with peanuts in it. Likewise, if something else is unhealthy for you, like oodles of hours playing video games, then you should also intentionally be careful about your screen time. Right? Or think about breakfast: Some medical researchers believe it is the most important meal of the day. They say it sets the tone for the way you'll eat and feel all day, even as it keeps your blood sugar stable and your energy up—that is, if you choose well.

Beware, though, living with intention is really hard work! One of the tricks to living with intention is to learn what's helpful and healthy for

you—and then sticking with those things. They will give you the kind of life you want. Not everyone wants the same kind of life, mind you! Goals are different for everyone. You won't have the same goals as the adults in your life, your siblings, or your friends. And that's part of what makes you unique!

So, what are your goals? Can you envision what you'll be like when you're a teenager or a young adult if you are already a teenager? How about being completely grown up? What kind of life do YOU want? You don't need an exact plan for the future. You don't need to know what career you'll choose, if you'll live on Earth or Mars, or if you'll drive a hover car or a space shuttle. It's okay if your goals are not specific. **Just having something to work toward makes it easier to know if you're on YOUR path.** For example, maybe you think you'd like to drive a car someday, help people in some way, help heal the planet, go to college or learn a trade, work with animals, or play the guitar really well. Those are all examples of worthy goals that will help you to stay the course on your "right life."

How to stay motivated

Something that's challenging for a lot of kids is not giving up as they strive to follow their dreams and be their best self. In other words, **staying motivated can be tough**. So, what's the key to staying the course? Let's look at two different scenarios.

Sarah really wanted a bike. All her friends had bikes. She wanted to ride around her neighborhood and bike to the lake. If she would clean her room every weekend for a month, her parents said they would buy her the bike. And that's what happened. Cool! She got her way, without a whole lot of effort on her part except for cleaning her room four times. No biggie. In this story, Sarah's goal came from outside her. Although her goal was getting a bike, her parents came up with the idea of her cleaning her room to achieve it AND her parents bought the bike for her. In other words, the idea as well as the "prize" came from her parents. When a goal comes from outside you, it's called **external motivation.** Here are some other examples of common external goals:

➡ **Getting something new**

➡ **Having dessert**

➡ **Earning TV or video game time**

➡ **Getting an allowance**

➡ **Hearing reassuring words from family members**

➡ **Becoming popular with other kids**

External goals are really good at motivating people for a short time, and that's okay. External motivation, however, goes away once you achieve or miss the goal. For example, do you think Sarah would have gotten her bike if she had been told she needed to clean her room for six months? Would she have stayed motivated over that long stretch of time? Probably not. Sarah would probably still be walking to the lake and to visit friends!

Luckily, there is another kind of motivation. It's called **internal motivation.** With internal motivation, you do something because it makes you feel good on the inside. Let's revisit Sarah and try a different outcome. Say Sarah's parents told her the bike was too expensive and they wouldn't pay for it. But she wanted that bike so badly that she decided to earn the money herself and got creative with ideas.

Over six months, Sarah helped neighbors to garden, sold lemonade on hot days, walked her aunt's dog, and even painted her grandparents' fence. Finally, when she had enough money, she had her parents take her to the store and she bought the bike. She felt awesome handing over the money she herself had earned. She felt good on the inside about achieving her goal, in large part because of her own planning, determination, persistence, and skill. **The magic of internal motivation is that it can keep you going for a long time.**

Perseverance *is being able to keep going despite difficulty and discomfort. It's not always easy to stay motivated. If you persevere, though, you can achieve your goal, or get close to it and pride yourself in the attempt!*

Your inner-critic ANTs: Real motivation stoppers!

Most of us have times when we really feel motivated, yet something gets in the way. Sometimes it's nothing big; it's just that we lose steam. At those times, we can usually start again and move forward. Other times, though, we get really bogged down by ANTs that judge us, ANTs that trigger our inner voice to be critical. When our "inner critic" kicks in, we need to tackle the ANTs that have taken over. Common ANTs that rob us of enthusiasm for and motivation to accomplish our goals include the following:

All-or-Nothing ANTs: It can take a long time to see progress on big ideas, and anyone could get discouraged. But All-or-Nothing ANTs make it really hard to see progress as it occurs. Instead, we get lost

in thinking: "I'll never get this done," "This will never work out," or "I always take on things I can't finish." Telling yourself "never" or "always" is a clue you are thinking this way.

Should ANTs: If you spend too much time telling yourself you should get to work on something, or you should be a better person, or you should save the world's animals, you may awaken an "inner rebel." It's natural to listen to all those Should ANTs and have an emotional reaction of resistance. It can begin to sound like you have someone bossy in your head giving you more tasks, instead of remembering that your goal was YOUR idea!

Jumping-to-Conclusions ANTs: Watch out for times when you get tired or weary and then predict you will end up failing. Everyone needs breaks when they're working on goals. So, notice when you jump to the conclusion you're going to fail and talk back to that ANT! You might remind yourself: "I've stuck with many goals until I succeeded." Can't think of any? Can you read this book? If you can, then reading is something you kept at, although learning to read is challenging.

Ignoring-the-Good ANTs: This ANT keeps you from seeing progress on your goals and causes you to forget to stop and praise yourself along the way. Controlling this ANT is vital to achieving your goals. The opposite of telling yourself, "I've barely done anything that counts" is to celebrate every little victory!

A key to dealing with all troublesome, motivation-stopping ANTs is being committed to the process more than to the outcome. Sometimes you don't reach your goal, yet you learn new things! Another tool for managing these ANTs is thinking about what you would say to your best friend in the same situation. Most of us are nice to friends but mean to ourselves. If you can come up with a helpful, encouraging replacement thought for your friend struggling with a goal, then you can say it to yourself. Easy peasy solution for all ANT issues!

HOW to Repair When You mess up

a s we've discussed before, it's also important not to let your fear of failure stop you from achieving your goals. Everyone makes mistakes. No one is perfect. It's by a grand design that we all mess up. **Mistakes are built into our humanness as a way to help us build our discernment.** "Discernment" is our ability to consider the options and make good decisions. When we make a mistake—and accept that mistake—we can learn not to repeat it.

When you have enough practice falling down and getting back up, or shifting from Plan A to Plan B, you often start hearing an encouraging inner voice. **That inner voice is your thinking FOR YOURSELF despite pressure from others or culture.** Over time, that inner voice becomes your "true North." You develop your ability to access and connect with your personal "inner compass" that points you toward positive behavior, living your values, and your right life.

Sometimes you might mess up royally. Everybody does! Maybe you were having a bad day, lost your temper, were really mean to another kid, pushed him, and broke a chair in the classroom when he fell over. What do you do then? You can admit to what you did and tell an adult. That adult can help you to **"make it right."** This means you fix

what you did, including acknowledging your mistreatment of another person, sincerely apologizing to that person, and even figuring out how to pay for the broken chair.

So, admit your mistakes. (EVERYONE makes them. They are a part of life!) Take responsibility for them. Apologize when someone else is impacted. This will make you a wiser, stronger person. In fact, some mistakes can end up sending you on your first step in a completely new direction—a better direction—where you discover something amazing. If you ignore or try to hide your mistakes, you can miss out on incredible opportunities. Truly, you are a work in progress, always changing and growing. You—the one and only you—can do whatever you choose to do! Sure, some things might not work out the way you anticipate. Just remember, though: Life is more about the journey than the destination!

Compassion for yourself is one of the quickest ways to find your way back to your right path! You might say quietly to yourself, "I know this is really hard, but I'm going to get through it."

Think about it!

Staying the Course

On the bottom-right side of the next page, in the "Goal" burst, write down something you are committed to achieving and the date by which you'd like to achieve that goal. In the stepping stones that start at the top of the page, write the things you will need to do to accomplish the goal. When can you finish the first step? Write a date above the stepping stone. What about the second step? Write a date above that stepping stone and so on, until all your stepping stones have dates above them. When you complete each stepping stone, you can cross it off and begin to "step" onto the next stone by doing what is written there until you reach the outcome you desire.

You will see that alongside the stepping stones is a space for you to list some mistakes or wrong turns on your journey to achieving your goal. Mistakes are no big deal! We learn from them if we remember them and do something different next time. So, note your mistakes and what you think you learned. That way you'll remember them and not repeat them.

Stepping Stones to Reaching My Goal

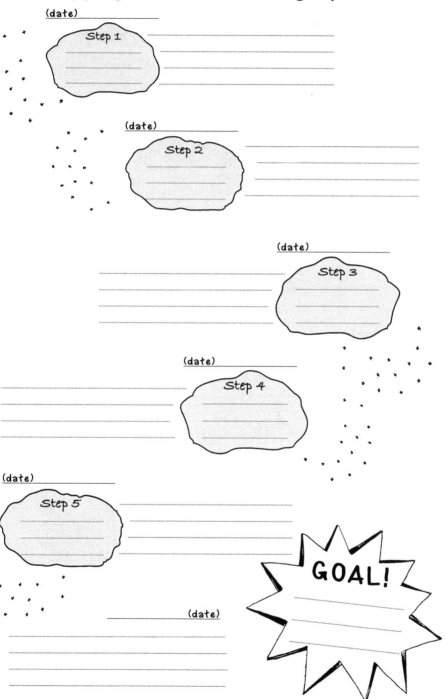

(date) _____

Step 1
_____ _____
_____ _____
_____ _____

(date) _____

Step 2
_____ _____
_____ _____
_____ _____

(date) _____

_____ Step 3
_____
_____ _____
_____

(date) _____

_____ Step 4
_____
_____ _____
_____

(date) _____

Step 5
_____
_____
_____

(date) _____

GOAL!
_____
_____
_____

SOMETHING I THOUGHT WAS A CHALLENGE FOR WHICH I'M NOW GRATEFUL IS...

Get Creative!

● **My Future Self!** On one side below, draw you as you are now. On the other side, draw you as the you who is graduating from high school. Label both drawings with descriptive words. What characteristics, traits, and values do you have right now? What characteristics, values, and skills would you like to have by the time you graduate from high school? Do you want to be patient? Compassionate? Hardworking? Funny? What things do you hope to have accomplished by the time you graduate? Will you have a summer job? Will you be able to drive? While you are drawing, spend some time thinking about the years between now and then. Seems like a long time, but you will be surprised at how fast it will go! Spend some time daydreaming while you draw about HOW you will become the teenager you want to become.

Me Now	Me as a High School Graduate

13 imaginal Discs & the Butterfly you are

You might know the general life cycle of a butterfly. It's something many of us are taught when we're very young. Remember? Butterflies are born as caterpillars. The caterpillars eat and eat until they're ready to make a cocoon for themselves. They hang out inside that cocoon for a period of time (usually between five and twenty-one days), going through extreme changes, called metamorphosis. Then they break out and . . . they're a butterfly! Wow, right? How did that little crawling, worm-like creature manage to turn into a gorgeous, flying butterfly? Clearly, it's magic! It is . . . and isn't. The caterpillar goes through a biological process—but even when there's a scientific explanation for something, it's no less magic, just magic we understand.

So, the caterpillar basically throws off everything that made it a caterpillar and sort of trades it in for butterfly parts. It becomes something entirely new. Except not really! The caterpillar doesn't somehow pull those beautiful wings out of thin air. The parts that turn a caterpillar into a butterfly were there the whole time! They are called **imaginal discs**. How fantastic is that? And so poetic. They sound like something you can imagine into being. What's important, though, is they're not imaginary.

Why is that important for YOU to know? Because you can think of yourself like a butterfly, but not in the sense of magically becoming a new person. Think of it this way: You are meant to be exactly the person you are right now. You are enough just as you are. Slowly, over time, though, different parts of yourself that were always there, hidden, will reveal themselves as you maintain your best of self and learn to use all your skills and smarts. In a way, YOU have your own version of imaginal discs! Not literally, as far as we know (otherwise we'd all be going into cocoons and sprouting wings a few weeks later), but **the essence of who you are and the only you who will ever be is with you always and always has been.** Interestingly, it's often when we're squeezed or uncomfortable in adversity that we grow the most.

Taking the butterfly metaphor one step further, consider that, to a butterfly, everything colorful looks like a flower. Sometimes she lands on something that isn't a flower, and she's shooed off. The butterfly doesn't get mad. The butterfly doesn't go and hide. The butterfly doesn't tantrum. What does the butterfly do? She simply flies off to the next colorful object, hoping it's a flower. So, if you get "shooed" by someone, consider acting like a butterfly. Don't take offense. Instead, wish that person well and move on to the next colorful thing that catches your eye or makes your heart sing. In fact, sometimes being shooed away simply helps to point us toward or keep us on our right path.

Staying with the butterfly theme, American mathematician and meteorologist Edward Lorenz posed the question, "Does the flap of a butterfly's wings in Brazil set off a tornado in Texas?" Called "The Butterfly Effect," this question got people thinking about the impact small changes can have. Seriously?! A butterfly causing a tornado!? It's just a theory, yet it's a cool metaphor.

Lorenz also wanted us to know that things are unpredictable. Another flap could do nothing at all. Likewise, human beings are unpredictable. Sometimes things may not go as you hope. Not every small action will have a major impact. If you keep trying, though, you just might inspire a tornado of love, kindness, good cheer, or compassion! The key is to keep embracing those imaginal discs—your best parts. The invitation is for you to be you.

> **individuality** *is the quality that makes one person different from all others. Everyone has it—even as we live in community and impact each other.*

Embracing You

When you accept your imaginal discs, it gives you freedom—to explore, to become your best self, to let go of things that no longer serve you (like the ANTs that give you low self-esteem and make you feel anxious or sad). Sure, moving from one stage of being you to being another version of you can be scary—and you might want to stay in your "cocoon" all the time. But what if caterpillars could keep things exactly as they are, maybe by taping up their cocoons every time they cracked before they were ready to be butterflies? Sadly, their wings would squeeze into a too-tight space and become damaged—and they might never learn what their wings were for!

An emerging butterfly has instinct on its side. It really doesn't need to trust that others won't laugh, pass judgments, or post on social media that it's wearing last year's wings. To become what it was meant to be, it has all the tools it needs. It has the science of its imaginal discs, which have been part of it all along, to ensure it will grow strong and be able to fly and outsmart the birds that would like it for lunch. The same goes for humans!

You were not born with the same instincts of a butterfly, but you were born to "fly," too. You were born to do YOU in your own unique way that brings your gifts to the world. Every person is a piece of the puzzle that makes up humanity. We need everyone's unique point of view, everyone's originality, everyone's creativity to improve our world. We need you. Yes, YOU! THE ONE AND ONLY YOU!

Your job as you grow up is to reveal your hidden gifts, accepting and inviting the best version of yourself—to become ridiculously YOU! Natural instincts won't ensure your full development as they do in butterflies. It's okay, though, because you still came into the world with everything you need to be a success. Your "imaginal discs" are already inside you, waiting to burst forth and enable you to fly. Don't let your ANTs keep you from becoming all you can be. Get your thoughts working for you, not against you. When that happens, oh, the many wonderful things you'll do!

Pause Point *After reading about your unique ways of being creative and smart and trapping some of your ANTs, consider what qualities of yours help you to soar. When you are feeling your best, what is it you are doing to create that feeling? What do you imagine you would like to create for yourself with your imaginal discs? Take a minute to write down on this date, today, what you want to remember about what you have learned.*

THOUGHTS & DOODLES

Think about it!

There is a story about a child who saw a butterfly struggling to get out of its cocoon. He wanted to help, so he pulled the cocoon apart for the butterfly. Sadly, because the butterfly didn't do the hard work of pushing against the cocoon with its new wings, its wings didn't get strong enough to ever be able to fly. Just as with the butterfly, WE, too, need the struggle, the practice, and the hard work to grow stronger and gain the skills to succeed in whatever we want to do.

Write down what you are "working on" now. Is it trying to be more patient? Are you learning how to play an instrument? Struggling with your throw-ins in soccer? Figuring out how to make some new friends? ALL of us are working on some aspect of ourselves, struggling and practicing something we're not quite skilled at YET. Just remember that your struggling isn't a problem. It's the stories you tell yourself and the expectations you set for yourself that make you want to quit or discourage you. The key is to not give up and know you'll be okay!

Once you identify what the something is you're working on, take a few minutes to write about how your struggle and hard work will help to improve that something and make you stronger in general.

_____

_____

_____

_____

_____

_____

_____

_____

_____

EVERYONE'S LIFE IS JUST THEIR OWN PERSONAL CLASSROOM. ONCE WE LEARN A LESSON, WE MOVE TO A DIFFERENT CLASSROOM. IT'S LIKE EVERYTHING THAT HAPPENS IN LIFE IS A SET-UP TO TEACH US TO BE OUR FULLEST AND BEST SELVES. EVEN THE SEEMINGLY DIFFICULT MOMENTS IN OUR LIFE PRESENT GROWTH OPPORTUNITIES AND OFFER US NEW TOOLS SO WE CAN BECOME OUR BEST SELF.

Dear Me! Picture yourself in a cocoon as a butterfly trying really hard to push out of the cocoon, struggling. Sometimes life feels challenging like that. What encouraging words would you like to hear to keep you going? What messages would make you continue to keep trying and make you feel as though you can do it? Write yourself a letter filled with words that will empower you. It might sound something like this:

Dear Me,

Sometimes things just feel gross. Know, though, that you will **FEEL THE SUN** on your skin again and **LOVE** what you love. Things might not go exactly how you'd like, but **YOU'RE GOING TO FIND YOUR WAY**. You're exactly who you're meant to be, and **YOU HAVE EVERYTHING YOU NEED TO THRIVE**. Trust yourself. **HAVE FUN**. Lighten up. Play that piano. I've got you!

Love, Me

When you finish your letter, put it in an envelope and address it to yourself. Then, ask an adult to put a stamp on the letter and mail it to you in a few months. Maybe it will arrive just when you need inspiration or motivation! You've got this!

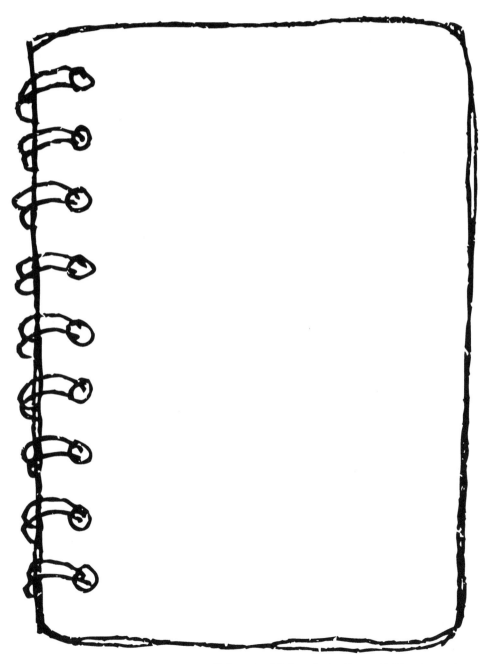

GROUP ENRICHMENT EXERCISES
Group Activities For Teachers, Counselors, Group Leaders, Parents, Supportive Adults, and Caregivers

A dults might facilitate the chapter activities suggested in the sections called "Think About It!" and "Get Creative!" In this special appendix to *The One and Only You*, however, I also offer experiential group activities as another way to explore and integrate the information presented in the chapters. My deepest thanks to educator extraordinaire Glenda Montgomery, a Certified Positive Discipline Lead Trainer, for her expertise and energy in writing, suggesting, and compiling these exercises, and to all those creators of the exercises who generously have permitted our reprinting them herein.

Chapter 1: FIRST THINGS FIRST: OWN YOU!

- **Discuss** all or part of the "Think About It!" questionnaire in a "Pair Share" with partners.

- **Do** the "Get Creative!" activity as a group art activity in class.

Alternatively, the two activities can be individually completed and then discussed as a group. The options for facilitation are numerous.

Chapter 2: HOW OTHER PEOPLE CAN HELP YOU DISCOVER YOU

WHAT IS IT?

Supplies: Poster paper, markers, and "items" written on separate sheets of paper

Prep Work: Write the following words on separate pieces of paper: **elephant tail, elephant trunk, elephant skin, elephant foot, and elephant ear.** Fold each paper in half to hide what's written on the paper.

Directions: Divide your group into five smaller groups of 2–5 people. Give each small group a half sheet of poster paper and a marker. Ask each group to choose a scribe. Then explain to the large group that each of the small groups will be given a folded piece of paper with the name of an object on it (the above "elephant" words). They are to list approximately 10–15 descriptive words on their poster about their object (what it looks like, how it feels, etc.). Tell them that, if they have never seen or felt their object, they may have to guess a bit. Tell them they will have only five minutes to come up with the descriptive words. Explain that the words on the folded papers are top secret and not to be said aloud. Then hand out the folded slips of paper with the elephant parts listed on them, one paper to each small group.

After five minutes, tell the groups to stop scribing, collect the posters, and hang them so that all can see them. Either have the descriptive words from each poster read aloud by a team member to the larger group or have every group move around the room to read each of the posters. Tell the students they are to make guesses inside their heads about what each item might be.

When everyone has had time to make some silent guesses about what each item might be, do the big reveal: Each group was describing THE SAME THING! Each group was describing an elephant. Process the discussion by asking questions:

- **Were** all the descriptions true?
- **Yet,** why were the descriptions so different?
- **Everyone** had only one piece of the puzzle, one "perspective." When we are getting to know someone or about something, do we always have the whole picture? The problem is, we often think we have more of the whole picture than we do.
- **Why** is staying curious important?
- **Why** do you think we did this activity?

Chapter 3: NO ONE IS PERFECT, BUT EVERYONE CAN BE CREATIVE

THINKING OUTSIDE THE BOX . . . *obtained on the Internet, available on many sites from many sources*

Directions: Below are nine dots arranged in a set of three rows. Your challenge is to draw four straight lines which go through the middle of all the dots without taking the pencil off the paper. If you are using a pencil, you must start from any position and draw the lines one after the other without taking your pencil off the page. Each line starts where the last line finishes. Remember, the instruction is to draw four straight lines to connect all the dots without taking your pencil off the paper.

Discussion: After giving the students a good amount of time to play with the puzzle, reveal the solution. For the solution, to connect the dots without lifting your pencil, you need to "think outside the box" . . . literally. Ask the students:

- **Why** do you think very few of us were able to solve this puzzle?
- **"Thinking** outside the box" is a saying you may have heard. What does it mean?
- **Why** do you think the ability to think outside the box is an important skill?

MAKING SOMETHING OLD NEW . . . *a well-loved game with many sources*

Prep Work: Collect a bunch of common items such as a broom, necktie, shoe, brick . . . anything.

Directions: Ask the children to stand in a circle. Explain to them that you are going to ask them to "think outside the box" and be creative. Tell them you are going to pass an object around the circle. When they are handed the object, they are to hold it, to say a way they could possibly use that item in a way that is different from its normal use, and then to pass it on to the person beside them. Allow the kids to be very creative. Perhaps the broom can be used as a fly swatter for a very large fly. Perhaps a shoe can be used to drink out of. It is acceptable to say "pass" and to pass the item on to the next person if a child can't think of something.

Go around the circle until the ideas seem to have run out for that object. Then, introduce a new object. Now that they have the swing of it, ask the students to take a step or two into the circle when it is their turn. When they say how they could use the object, have them act it out at the same time.

This game gets easier as the creative juices start flowing. There is much laughter, too. If they get very good at this game, the children can act out the new use of the item and the rest of the group can guess what the new use is before the object is passed along.

Chapter 4: YAH, BOO, UGH, GRRR: UNDERSTANDING EMOTIONS

EMOTION EXPLORATION

Prep Work: Copy the handout on the next page.

Supplies: Handout and poster paper on an easel or a dry erase board

Directions:

Step #1: Tell the children, "Emotions themselves are not always positive or always negative. In some circumstances, they can be helpful; in others, they can be hurtful. Then, write "Afraid" on the board or paper. Draw a line down the middle of the paper, vertically under the word. Ask the class, "When might being afraid be a helpful thing?" Write down their answers. Then ask, "When might being afraid be negative?" Write down those answers on the other side of the line. Discuss the responses.

Step #2: Give out the handout. Ask the students to find a partner and complete it. Stress that everyone's answers may be different and that is okay. Have them talk about each answer with their partner and share ideas, exploring how the ideas are similar and different. Then, bring the class back together to discuss two or three more emotions as you explored being "afraid" with the class, considering when the emotions are helpful and when they are not helpful. Be very open to what the students say. This is not a "right/wrong" discussion.

The Power of Labeling Emotions

According to research by Matthew Leiberman *et al.*, recognizing and naming our difficult emotions has a physiologically calming effect on our brains and bodies. Also, the more familiar we are with our emotions—and words to describe them—the more effective we will be at self-regulation. So teach your students the powerful strategy of labeling emotions. Especially when discussing things that may trigger anxiety and other disturbing feelings, it's helpful to include movement and mindfulness. There are many supportive regulation strategies you might utilize before, during, and as closure to the lessons included in this book; some resources are on pages 199-200.

EMOTION EXPLORATION

When might each of these emotions be negative? When could they be positive? Go through each emotion answering these questions. Find a friend and discuss how your answers are similar and different.

Emotion	Negative	Positive
angry		
bored		
cheerful		
embarrassed		
excited		
grateful		
guilty		
happy		
included		
inspired		
loving		
sad		
worried		

Chapter 5: TAKE THAT ANTs!

CONCRETIZING THE CONCEPTS

Lead a discussion about the chapter's concepts. Then, divide a poster in two parts, drawing a line vertically down the middle. At the top of the first column, write "ANT . . . automatic negative thought." At the top of the second column, write, "GET REAL." Ask the group to pick a particular ANT and then brainstorm true, realistic thoughts that might be more helpful to have. Write down all the ideas. Repeat this with a few more ANTs, so the children see that each ANT can be replaced with more positive, balanced thoughts. When they understand and have practiced this skill, then play the following game. (In real life, we don't harm any living creature! Even ants play a role in our ecosystem and are important to the world.)

ANT SQUASHING GAME

Prep Work: Write in marker a common ANT on each of six or more index cards. Examples could be:

- I work too slowly.
- I am not smart enough.
- I am not brave enough.
- They will never be my friends. I won't even try.
- Oh! That would be embarrassing. I am not going to try that.
- I will probably just make a mistake. If I can't do it right, it isn't worth doing.

Directions: Read aloud what you have written on each card. Ask the kids if they have ever had ANTs like this negative self-talk that bugs them. Ask for suggestions of what other ANTs might bug kids. Write their suggestions on additional index cards in marker, one per card. Shuffle the cards. Explain the game.

The Game: A volunteer comes up to the front of the room or the middle of a circle, draws a card from the pack, and then says, in a voice this ANT might use, whatever is written on the card. Whoever thinks they have a true, realistic thought to balance out the ANT and "squash" it raises a hand. The volunteer chooses someone. That person says what an effective realistic thought would be, and, in reaction to this thought, the volunteer throws the index card (ANT) on the ground and stomps on it. The person who offered the realistic thought can then grab an index card and say the next ANT the way it might talk. Continue the game for as long as the ideas flow.

Chapter 6: SOMETIMES "BEING GREEN" ISN'T EASY

POTATO ACTIVITY . . . *with thanks to Dr. Patreese D. Ingram, from her* More Diversity Activities for Youth and Adults, *available at https://extension.psu.edu/more-diversity-activities-for-youth-and-adults*

Objective: To help youth eliminate stereotyping and recognize the uniqueness of each individual

Supplies: Brown paper bag, one potato for each student in the class, and one potato for the teacher

Directions: Select one potato for your demonstration and have a story in mind to describe your potato to the class. Hold up your potato in front of the class and say, "I have here a potato. I don't know about you, but I've never thought that much about potatoes. I've always taken them for granted. To me, potatoes are all pretty much alike. Sometimes I wonder if potatoes aren't a lot like people."

Pass around the bag of potatoes and ask each student to take one potato. Tell each student to "examine your potatoes, get to know its bumps, scars, and defects and make friends with it for about one minute or so in silence. Get to know your potato well enough to be able to introduce your 'friend' to the group."

After a few minutes, tell students that you'd like to start by introducing your "friend" to them. Then share a creative, made-up story about your potato and how it got its bumps. Now, tell students that the class would like to meet their "friends." Ask who will introduce their "friend" first. Ask for several, if not all, to tell the group about their potatoes.

When enough students have introduced their "friends" to the class, take the bag around to each person. Have them put their "friends" back into the bag. Then, ask the class, "Would you agree with the statement 'all potatoes are the same'? Why or why not?"

Next, mix up the potatoes and roll them out onto a table. Ask everyone to come up and pick out their potatoes. After everyone has their potatoes and you have your "friend" back, say, "Well, perhaps potatoes are a little like people. Sometimes, we lump people of a group all together. When we think, 'They're all alike,' we are really saying that we haven't taken the time or thought it important enough to get to know the person. When we do, we find out everyone is different and special in some way, just like our potato friends."

Discussion: Ask students to think about groups at school or in the community that we tend to lump together. If they have trouble thinking of groups, you may want to prompt them with some of the following groups:

- **kids in band**
- **kids of a certain religion**
- **kids in the gifted classes**
- **kids in special education classes**
- **kids from a certain racial or ethnic group**
- **kids who live in apartments or trailers**
- **all the girls**
- **all the boys**
- **all kids who identify as "they/their"**

Use groups that are relevant and meaningful for the school/community you are addressing. Then, discuss answers to the following questions:

1. **When** we lump everyone from the same group together and assume they all have the same characteristics, what are we doing? What is this called?

2. **Do** you know a lot of people from the groups we tend to lump together? Do they all fit the stereotype?

3. **Why** are stereotypes dangerous?

Chapter 7: FEELING GOOD ABOUT YOURSELF

CLASSROOM (OR HOME/FAMILY/GROUP) VALUES

Have the children brainstorm a list of the commonly agreed upon values of their classroom or home/family/group. This can be an activity by itself and may be enough for one session.

A follow-up activity could be, in a separate place/poster, to have the kids brainstorm a list of adjectives that would be against or the opposite of the group's values. This list might include words such as mean, unsafe, selfish, rude, disrespectful, and impatient. Once you have the list, ask the kids, as an example to work with, to choose one of these ways of behaving that undermines the group values. Then, ask for an example of a fictional situation in which someone might be acting against that group value and may want other kids to as well. Then start discussing the question, "In this situation, what could we do to stay true to our group values?"

Yet a further extension of this activity is acting it out. Have the kids brainstorm several different options and then act out the scenarios. Start with two or three volunteering to be the actors. Make sure the actors know which characters they are in this fictional drama. When a point arrives in the drama when an observing student feels he/she/they can enter the scene and use one of the brainstormed ideas, he/she/they can yell, "Freeze!" The action and talk then freezes until the student is in the scene and begins talking. The others play along with the new student's prompts. You can replay this drama many times, allowing different students to play different roles until all the brainstormed ideas for how to stay true to our values are exhausted and many different values-undermining scenarios are portrayed.

Chapter 8: BEING MAD AND SAD

LANDSCAPES OF OUR LIVES

Supplies: Clay, play dough, or Sculpey; toothpicks; paper; tape

Directions: Have the kids create a scene of mountains with a deep valley or canyon between them using clay, play dough, or Sculpey. Then have them create several flags by taping paper pieces about the size of a fortune cookie to toothpicks. Divide the flags into two groups. On each of the flags in one group, have them write one super happy time in their life. On each of the flags in the other group, have them write a different sad time in their life. Once they have a handful of flags, instruct them to plant the "happy times" flags on top of the mountains and the "sad times" flags in the canyons or valleys. Then lead them in a discussion with comments such as, "Everyone's lives have mountain tops and valleys. Everyone's lives have happy times and sad. These are the landscapes of our lives that make our unique life landscapes."

THE ATTITUDE OF GRATITUDE: FILLING OUR CUP

Explain to your young friends that social scientists have been studying what makes happy people happy for many years. They have discovered some really interesting things. One discovery is that happy people tend to be very grateful people. They take time to recognize what they have. They are thankful for even the small things and make a practice of saying so. They look at a glass and say, "That glass is half full!" instead of "That glass is half empty!"

Create a poster with the outline of a large cup or glass on it. Give everyone in the class a few sticky notes. Ask them to think of things for which they are grateful. Ask them to write one thing for which they are grateful on each sticky note. Starting at the bottom of the drawn cup, have the kids stick their "gratitudes" side by side on your poster side, trying to "fill the cup" with gratitude. Take time each day to pull a few gratitudes from the cup and read them aloud. Then put them back. For research on the link between gratitude and happiness, check out:

- Fabian Gander, Rene T. Proyer, Willibald Ruch, and Tobias Wyss. "Strength-Based Positive Interventions: Further Evidence for Their Potential in Enhancing Well-Being and Alleviating Depression," *Journal of Happiness Studies* 14, no. 4 (August 2013): 1241-59, DOI 10.1007/s10902-012-9380-0.
- Martin Seligman. *Flourish: A Visionary New Understanding of Happiness and Well-Being*. New York: Free Press, 2011.
- N.L. Sin and S. Lyubomirsky. "Enhancing Well-Being and Alleviating Depressive Symptoms with Positive Psychology Interventions," *Journal of Clinical Psychology* 65, no. 5 (2009): 467–87.

Note: Other social science research points clearly to physical activity and being with friends as ways to remain happy. Think of fun, simple games you can play WITH your class that have you out of breath and laughing while you play!

Chapter 9: ANXIETY, WORRY, & PANIC, OH, MY!

WHAT IS THE WORST THAT CAN HAPPEN?

In combination with the "Try a Wacky Approach" exercise on page 136, read the book *Could Be Worse!* by James Stevenson to the kids with exaggeration, to bring humor to the subject of anxiety and worry. Ask the students why they think you read this book to them. If they don't come up with these answers, bring up the following ideas: Our anxieties and worries are often overblown. Sometimes something we think is going to be bad turns out to be good. Also, using humor when we are worried can be helpful, because we really can't control what happens in the future.

WHAT HAPPENS WHEN WE CAN'T SHAKE THE WORRY?

Sometimes it's challenging to handle big emotions. Have students work in small groups, each with a large piece of paper and some markers. Ask each group to make a list of approximately six ways they know to calm down when they have experienced big emotions such as worry, anger, or disappointment. When the groups have their lists completed, post them around the classroom. Then have the students move from poster to poster around the classroom with a marker and place a checkmark after all the suggestions they know work for them and the ones they think would work for them. Afterward, lead a discussion about "self-regulation," the ability to monitor and manage your emotions and emotional responses. Explain that the strategies they came up with are all self-regulation practices that can keep them feeling calm or help them to calm down when upset. From the students' posters, create one poster of the most popular strategies to leave up as a resource. End with the idea that, if emotions are too overwhelming even with trying some self-regulation strategies—it's important to tell a caring adult.

MINDFULNESS AND SELF-REGULATION ACTIVITIES

This is an excellent time to begin to teach more self-regulation and mindfulness activities. Just a few have been included here, but many more can be found by doing a Google search.

Square Breathing: First demonstrate square breathing without explanation. Then invite the kids to join you. Tell them they are going to use their pointer fingers as imaginary pencils to draw an imaginary square in the air in front of them while they breathe in and out. Then say, "As you breathe in slowly, draw your line up. When you get to the top (counting silently one, two), hold your breath as you move your finger to the right and complete the drawing of the top of your box to the count of two. When you get to where the line is going to be drawn down, slowly let out your air, or breathe out, to the count of two. And, when you reach the bottom of your breath, hold it and draw the rest of your box so your drawing of a square is complete."

After leading the group with the instructions, just count the box sides as they continue the practice, saying, "Breathe in, one, two; Hold, one, two; Breathe out, one, two; Hold, one two; etc." Another variation of the square breathing mindfulness practice is to have the kids close their eyes while doing it.

Birthday Candles: Ask the children to put up the number of fingers that correspond to their age. Then have them pretend these fingers are birthday candles. Explain that, with each candle that is "blown out," they can focus on one wish they have for themselves, for their families, classmates, school, or whomever they want. The idea is to take time with each candle. When the candle is "blown out," that finger goes down, and a new breath blows out a new candle with a new wish.

Can You Hear It? Tell the kids you're going to ring a chime. (Some chimes are better than others for this activity, so experiment with a few before choosing a chime with a quality tone that will last.) Once you ring the chime, invite the kids to close their eyes and put up their hands when they can no longer hear even a hint of the chime's sound in the air.

Body Check In: Explain to the group that we're often so busy we forget to check in with ourselves. In other words, we get focused *outside* and forget about how we are doing *inside*.

Tell them you're going to lead them in a "body check-in," but that they can do this for themselves any time. This activity tends to calm, ground, and refresh people. It also teaches us to pay attention to the messages our physical bodies offer. Also, let the kids know this will be a silent check-in, that when you ask questions, they will be answering in their minds, silently. Note: If you are introducing mindfulness to your class for the first time, you may want to do check-ins with only one body part at a time and slowly combine them as the kids get used to this type of silent check-in.

To start, ask the students to sit comfortably with their feet on the floor. Then invite them to close their eyes and really be curious as they check in with each body part. Start with the feet. Ask them to check in with them, to feel the floor, to feel their feet in their shoes. Continue asking leading questions such as, "How are your feet feeling? Are they sore? Comfortable? What about your ankles? How about your calves and shins? How are they feeling? Are they calm? Are they jumpy?" and so forth. Keep asking students to check in and notice—without judgment, just with curiosity—moving through the upper legs, stomach, back, chest, arms, and hands, until you reach their heads. When you've asked about the whole body, direct the kids to open their eyes and share how they feel differently now than before the scan.

Chapter 10: YOUR SHIELD: IS IT REAL? IS IT KIND?

WE HAVE YOUR BACK

Comment: By this time, your group is connected by the activities in the book. This activity is the antithesis of the "shield." It is about our vulnerable backs and our all wanting to know we "have each other's backs."

Objectives: To inspire participants to be encouraged as well as to foster a sense of belonging and significance

Supplies: Safety pins or good masking tape, card stock paper, and markers

Prep Work: Have a space cleared of tables and chairs so the kids can gather as a group, standing together.

Directions: As they enter the room, with a safety pin or masking tape (safety pin is better), attach a piece of cardstock paper to the back of each child, hand everyone a marker, and direct them to stand together in the open space. Just this gets the fun going!

Once everyone is in the room, explain, "We have gotten to know one another pretty well in this class. We have shared both our traumas and our triumphs. Each of you brings a great deal to this class. Look around the room at one another. When you look, you may remember something about each one, something shared, something you know about that person that makes a positive difference in this class. When I say 'go,' write a positive characteristic or trait you associate with that person on the card on that person's back. Once you do that, move to another person and write a positive word or group of words you associate with that person. Continue until you have written on everyone else's back."

When everyone is done, have the kids help one another detach the cards from each other's back. Then, have them silently read what others wrote about them—or aloud if you have the time. If the participants read aloud on the spot, the activity can be left like this. Alternatively, after a few moments of allowing the silent reading of their messages, you might lead a group discussion, asking, "What came out of this activity for you? How might it affect future discouragement for you? How might it make you stronger? What surprised you?"

Chapter 11: THE POWER OF COMPASSION

STEP INTO MY SHOES . . . *thanks to Melanie Miller, school counselor and Certified Positive Discipline Trainer*

Objective: For students to become aware of their classmates' "worlds," ultimately encouraging understanding and tolerance

Prep Work: Prepare six to eight "shoe boards" on poster board. Each poster board will have outlines of two feet with a descriptive "label" identifying the particular set of "shoes." For example, you might use the following labels:

I'm Overscheduled Shoes:

My Parents are Getting a Divorce Shoes:

I feel alone. No one else is dealing with this. I feel angry. I feel confused. I'm tired of my parents arguing. Is it my fault? I miss my friends when I go to my dad's house. Everyone in my family is so angry. I just wish my parents would get back together. It's hard to concentrate at school.

I'm Always Picked On Shoes:
> I don't have any friends. Kids make fun of me. I feel scared. I don't like school. I wish adults would take me seriously. I try to fit in. I sometimes do things that people tell me to just to make a friend. I feel alone. I wish I could disappear.

Bystander Shoes:
> I want to be a part of the cool group. If I tell an adult, will I be next? I feel worried. I feel confused. Sometimes the teasing is funny. I belittle people. I join in. I want to have friends. I don't want to be the next victim. The power feels good. At least I'm not the one getting picked on.

New Kid at School Shoes: I just moved here and don't know anyone. I sit alone at lunch. No one asks me to play at recess. I miss my old friends and school. I feel alone. I feel depressed. No one understands. Other kids look at me and talk behind my back.

Excluded Kid Shoes: I walk up to a group and they walk away from me. Others spread rumors about me. No one invites me to their group. When I sit down at lunch, others move away from me. I feel alone. I feel embarrassed. I wish someone would notice me, talk to me. Kids laugh at me. They do things behind my back.

Perfect Student Shoes: I have to get perfect grades. I need other kids to like me. I'll do anything to impress others. I feel nervous and anxious. If they only knew what my life is really like. My parents expect me to get really good grades. I have to be the best athlete. There is no room for being mediocre in my family. My parents don't understand. I feel so much pressure. I can't keep up much longer.

Bully Shoes: I hurt others because I feel hurt. My brother is mean to me. I feel powerless. My dad doesn't have time for me. I need to look cool. I feel discouraged. My friends/I think I'm funny. Tough is better than weak. I'll get even. Underneath the toughness I feel vulnerable. My mom yells at me. I'll hurt you before you hurt me. I didn't know what I did was being mean or bullying.

Directions:

1. **Arrange** the shoe boards in a circle on the floor.

2. **Ask** for six to eight volunteers to participate. Instruct participants to pick one shoe board to stand on. Remind all students, participants, and audience that this is a quiet activity. There is to be no talking.

3. **As** participants stand on their shoe board, ask them to be fully present in their "shoes." Ask them to read silently what is written on their board. Encourage them to notice what they're feeling, what they're thinking, and what they're deciding about themselves and others. Process with questions such as, "What is it like to step into these shoes?"

4. **After** a few minutes of reflection, ask the participants to move on to the next pair of shoes. Encourage them to continue to move around the circle stepping into each pair of shoes when they're ready. Again, ask them to be fully present in each pair of shoes. Students can signal they are ready to move on to the next board by stepping off their current board and quietly waiting for the person before them to move on.

5. **Once** students have completed all the boards, ask them to stop. Perhaps let other kids step into the shoes until everyone has had the opportunity to participate. Then, process the experience with them. You might want to explore the following questions:

- **How** many pairs of shoes do you have at home? Does anyone have just one pair and have to wear them all the time?
- **How** do you decide which pair you are going to wear? For example, "They're cool, look good with an outfit, keep me dry in wet weather, keep me warm in the snow, are okay for PE days, help me run fast," and so on.) Note: Our shoes fulfill a purpose—just like our behavior does: to get a sense of love and belonging, contribution, and more.
- **How** can you tell if a pair of shoes no longer fits?
- **What** do you do when your shoes no longer fit, are out of style, are worn out, and so forth? How do you decide what kind of shoes you need to buy? Who helps you find a pair that fits?

Through the metaphor of shoes, students learn they can move in and out of roles and, when a role doesn't fit anymore, they can find their own personal power or ask for help to move away from what isn't working for them to something more encouraging.

Chapter 12: YOU CAN DO IT!

SUPERHEROES! . . . *created by Glenda Montgomery based on the research of social psychologist Amy Cuddy who found that power posing results in feelings of increased self-confidence. Check out Amy Cuddy's work at: ted.com/talks/amy_cuddy_your_body_language_may_shape_who_you_are.*

PART ONE: SUPERHERO POSING

Directions: After a song or something energizing and fun together (maybe immediately after recess), ask the kids to think about superheroes and invite them to say the names of their favorite superheroes in a popcorn brainstorm. Remind the students that all superheroes seem to have a pose they make when they are really feeling their power. Explain that, on your cue, you will all yell together, "3, 2, 1, SUPERHERO!" jump from your chairs, and strike a superhero pose that you will all hold together for about ten seconds, feeling the power! Make sure you join in, as it will be much more fun (and powerful) with you! Afterward, ask how the kids felt after the superhero pose compared to before.

Then, ask them to personalize the superhero pose so that it is their very own pose. Invite them to think about what would make a great superhero pose just for them. Ask who is willing to share their unique superhero pose. Have several students share.

Now, use those poses all together. Explain that, this time, everyone will yell, "3, 2, 1, I AM a superhero!" and strike their unique superhero pose and hold it for ten seconds.

PART TWO: REVIEW OF GIFTS

Directions: Now that everyone has a powerful pose, invite the class to settle back into their chairs and think of all each of them has learned while reading and doing the activities of the book. Review the chapters by writing the chapter headings out where the students can see them. Ask the students to jot down some things they learned or discovered about their superpower gifts as they worked through this book. You might want to give everyone a handout with the chapters listed with lines beneath for the notes they jot on each chapter. You also might need to help them remember the content and activities of each chapter.

Chapter 1: First Things First: Own You!
Chapter 2: How Other People Can Help You Discover You
Chapter 3: No One Is Perfect, But Everyone Can
       Be Creative
Chapter 4: Yay, Boo, Ugh, Grrr: Understanding Feelings
Chapter 5: Take That Ants!
Chapter 6: Sometimes "Being Green" Isn't Easy
Chapter 7: Feeling Good About Yourself
Chapter 8: Being Mad and Sad
Chapter 9: Anxiety, Worry, & Panic, Oh, My!
Chapter 10: Your Shield: Is It Real? Is It Kind?
Chapter 11: The Power Of Compassion
Chapter 12: You Can Do It!
Chapter 13: Imaginal Discs & the Butterfly You Are

PART THREE: SUPERHERO!

Directions: After the students have collected some ideas about their own personal learning on at least most of the chapters, present the following Superman introduction, using a loud, dramatic radio announcer's voice: "Faster than a speeding bullet! More powerful than a locomotive! Able to leap tall buildings in a single bound! It's a bird. It's a plane. No! It's SUPERMAN!"

Ask the students to think of what each of them is good at and to create a similar Superhero introduction. The introduction should end in,

" It's a _____
It's a _____
No! It's SUPER_____!' "
with the last blank filled in with the student's name.

Pass out paper and tell the students they have 15 minutes and to work in pairs to come up with the introduction for each of them, along the same lines as Superman's but unique to each of them. The introductions do not have to be perfect.

When the 15-minute writing period is up, explain they are going to take turns introducing their partner while their partner does his or her superhero pose. Ask the "announcer" to sit while the superhero stands in his/her/their pose. This will get noisy, but have all the superheroes stay in their pose while the announcers read the introductions. Then, have them switch so everyone gets a chance to pose and to read a partner's introduction.

At the end, ask if anyone would like to share his/her/their pose and introduction with the class. Ask if the student would like his/her/their introduction read by the partner or by you, the adult leader. Be sure to use a dramatic radio announcer's voice for the introduction.

Then, see if anyone else would like to share.

Chapter 13: IMAGINAL DISCS & THE BUTTERFLY YOU ARE

BE THE BUTTERFLY

Supplies: Letter-size card stock for each child, various magazines for cutting apart, glue sticks, Mod Podge

Prep Work: For each student, draw the outline of a butterfly on card stock. Have many types of magazines available for students to find images to which they are drawn—images that might represent their "imaginal discs," the parts of themselves (including interests, talents, environments, skills, and ways of life) that make them unique.

Directions: Ask the students to rip or cut images out of the magazines to which they "are drawn" and then to use glue sticks to create a collage, completely filling the wings of their butterfly outline. Once finished, use Mod Podge to seal the collages. When the collages dry, ask the students to share with a partner what's on their butterfly's wings. You may also want to hang the butterflies from the ceiling in a way that, when students look up, they can see the colorful part of the butterflies facing down at them.

NOTES

1. Nicole Jon Sievers and Norene Gonsiewski, "Your Brain: Your Greatest Asset," in *It's Your Mind: Own It!* (Portland, OR: Innovations Press, 2015), 10–25.

2. "The Limbic System," Queensland Brain Institute, University of Queensland, accessed July 22, 2020, https://qbi.uq.edu.au/brain/brain-anatomy/limbic-system.

3. Kerryn Neulinger et al, "Prospective Memory and Frontal Lobe Function," *Aging, Neuropsychology, and Cognition* 23, no. 2 (2016): 171–83, https://pubmed.ncbi.nlm.nih.gov/26212653/; and "Lobes of the Brain," Queensland Brain Institute, University of Queensland, accessed July 22, 2020, https://qbi.uq.edu.au/brain/brain-anatomy/lobes-brain

4. Cèline Chayer and Morris Freedman, "Frontal Lobe Functions," *Current Neurology and Neuroscience Reports* 1, no. 6 (2001): 547–52, doi: 10.1007/s11910-001-0060-4.

5. Sivapriya Ramamoorthy and John A. Cidlowski, "Corticosteroids— Mechanisms of Action in Health and Disease," *Rheumatic Disease Clinics of North America* 42, no. 1 (February 2016): 15–31, https://www.ncbi.nlm.nih.gov/pmc/articles/PMC4662771/.

6. Brent A. Vogt, "Pain and Emotion Interactions in Subregions of the Cingulate Gyrus," *Nature Reviews Neuroscience* 6, no. 7 (July 2005): 533–44, doi:1038/nrn1704.

7. "Hypothalamas," MedlinePlus, U.S. National Library of Medicine, accessed July 22, 2020, https://medlineplus.gov/ency/article/002380.htm.

8. "Amygdala," Encyclopedia Britannica, accessed July 22, 2020, https://www.britannica.com/science/amygdala.

9. "Diseases That Affect the Hippocampus," Medical News Today, accessed July 22, 2020, https://www.medicalnewstoday.com/articles/313295.

10. Shazia Veqar Siddique et al, "Neuropsychology of Prefrontal Cortex," *Indian Journal of Psychiatry* 50, no. 3 (2008): 202–208, http://www.indianjpsychiatry.org/article.asp?issn=0019-5545;year=2008;volume=50;issue=3;spage=202;epage=208;aulast=Siddiqui.

11. "The Pleasure Centres," The Brain from Top to Bottom, accessed July 22, 2020, http://thebrain.mcgill.ca/flash/d/d_03/d_03_cr/d_03_cr_que/d_03_cr_que.html.

GRATEFUL

My sincerest gratitude goes to Ruthie Matinko-Wald, the wordsmith who synthesized tons of ideas into a cohesive whole; her devotion to producing books that positively change the world is admirable. Illustrator Darcy Cline's humanitarian values made it a joyful breeze to collaborate on this project. Norene Gonsiewski added invaluable insight and wisdom; I so appreciate and applaud her making the world a more compassionate place.

I'd also like to recognize: Juliana Weiss-Roessler, who helped me to pull initial ideas together; thank you for making my scribbles go further. Dr. Andy Benjamin, who reminded me of my values. Glenda Montgomery, Jane Johnston, and Monique Terner, all stellar educators committed to helping youth; they each gave excellent input and feedback on various drafts. Dr. Diaz who reminded me about butterflies. Charles, T, Amy, Rebecca, Sarah, Steph, Jules, Sherry, Adrian, Michelle, Mandy, and Deb—my front-row cheerleaders who make life more beautiful. Tanya Maxine Senn, who is closer to a saint than anyone I know; your support and unconditional love radiate through my and my children's lives. Linda Carroll, my mom, who taught me to dig deep and move forward in service. My godmother, Annie, who inspires the best in everyone. My sisters, Jaimee and Courtney, from both of whom I learned that everything is possible and to lead with humor and love. My dad, Frank Rodriguez, and my brothers—Josh, Tobias, and Daniel—who are all kind and wise men for whom I am ever grateful. My sons Gabriel, Nicholas, Jacob, Benjamin, and Maxwell are my heart; they always inspire me to do better and more.

Finally, my husband, Eric Louis Sievers MD, is the most devoted soul I know. A human who loves science and life itself, he is forever chasing a cure for cancer or clothing, sheltering, or feeding an abandoned child he will never meet, working to improve living conditions for humans and animals alike. He has put countless hours and resources into our family's two nonprofits, supporting my every fleeting (and enduring) idea and desire with a solid foundation. I am eternally in awe of his innate goodness and willingness to work for what is right and helpful.

MEET THE AUTHOR

Nicole (Cole) Jon Sievers, MSW, LCSW, is an innovative problem solver, speaker, licensed clinical social worker, educator, social justice advocate, and co-author (with Norene Gonsiewski) of the award-winning *It's Your Mind: Own it! A Manual for Every Teen.* For over thirty years, she has worked with youth and the systems serving them. Her diverse roles have included therapist, teacher, educational district consultant, Outward Bound instructor, and forensic consultant.

Nicole is the founder and executive director of Stand for Courage (standforcourage.org). This bullying-prevention program employs stories, creativity, and popular culture to recognize students leading bystander action to eradicate bullying. In 2014, the SFC school-based program was honored by the American Psychological Association with a Visionary Award. In 2017, an academic study reported that victimization decreased by 69 percent when schools implemented SFC bullying-prevention practices. Building on her bullying prevention work, Nicole also served as a producer for the IndieFlix documentary *The Upstanders*, about the bystander's role in bullying prevention.

Nicole also is the co-founder of Little Mercies (littlemercies.org), a nonprofit creating channels for simple kindness and for the distribution of essentials to ease the suffering of children living in the world's harshest conditions. The current focus of Little Mercies is migrant children awaiting court dates in U.S. border towns and Burmese refugee children in Thailand. An important component of Little Mercies is youth supporting youth. Little Mercies' backpack program has delivered close to 3,000 backpacks filled with essential items. Many of these have been collected by youth and filled by youth.

Also an avid supporter of the arts, Nicole served on the Seattle Music Commission from 2014 to 2019. She also is an Advisory Board member of the Origins Project Foundation, which strives to address the challenges of the 21st century through public events with thought leaders.

Nicole lives in La Jolla, California. She and her husband, Eric, are the grateful parents of five sons, two large dogs, and a cat.

MEET THE ILLUSTRATOR

Darcy Cline is an illustrator, graphic designer, and artist with a career spanning over thirty years.

She studied graphic design and art at Central Washington University, The Art Institute of Seattle, and Pierce College, where she won Art Student of the Year and discovered the Student Life programs. This connection led to working with design and international students as a designer/mentor with Pierce College Student Life and Tacoma Community College Office of Student Engagement.

From 2001-2010 Darcy led mission trips to La Gloria, Mexico, with Esperanza. Through this organization's programs, high school and college students spend a week building community and cinder-block homes with families in the towns of Tijuana County.

Darcy also led student trips to work with the people of the Crow Reservation in Billings, Montana, and with migrant farm workers of Lynden, Washington. All these mission trips were community-building and learning-based experiences.

Darcy is the proud mother of four grown children and two grandchildren. She lives in Washington State with her husband, two rescue pups, and an abandoned cat who adopted the family.

By Nicole Jon Sievers MSW
and Norene Gonsiewski MSW

Adolescence isn't easy. But this must-read book can help every teen have an awesome life. It's also an invaluable support for parents of teens and anyone who cares about them!

Offering up-to-date information and practical tools based on neuroscience, the authors inspire readers to understand their thoughts and feelings, master strategies for dealing with challenges and setbacks, and embrace their unique creativity. Every chapter is filled with clever illustrations, spot-on examples, and helpful enrichment exercises. Ultimately, the book challenges youth to own their minds, find their inner power, and create a life they love.

It Starts with a Backpack

Vulnerable migrant children living in squalid shelters along the US–Mexico border. Burmese refugee children struggling to survive along Thailand's border. These defenseless children are not mistakes. Every single one of them is as important as you and me—and they need our help.

How? By supporting the work of Little Mercies, a nonprofit dedicated to easing the suffering of children living in the world's harshest conditions and fleeing from unspeakable hardships and violence.

- **For Burmese refugee children, cash donations will provide food, medical care, and education.**
- **Pack a backpack with "essential" items and mail it to Little Mercies for getting into the hands of migrant children. Better yet, organize a school-wide collection!**

Essential items:

Art supplies	New socks & underwear
Band aids	Non-perishable, ready-to-eat snacks
Blanket	Skin-cleansing wipes
Children's book in Spanish	Small flashlight
Coloring book	Stuffed animal/toy
Comb/brush	Toothbrush/toothpaste
Hand sanitizer	Travel-size shampoo/conditioner/
Journal or small notebook	body wash

currency that matters

For details and more information:
LittleMercies.org
nicolejonsievers@gmail.com